PENSACOLA'S FINEST:

THE STORY OF THE **PENSACOLA POLICE DEPARTMENT**

MIKE SIMMONS

© Copyright 2020 by Michael Simmons — All rights reserved.

It is not legal to reproduce, duplicate, or transmit any part of this document in either electronic means or printed format. Recording of the publication is strictly prohibited.

DEDICATION

Writing a book takes a lot of hours. And it takes a lot of focus…and encouragement. To give time and focus to one thing takes away from something else. For my book I took time away from my best friend and wife, Jerri. She selflessly allowed her time to be used for the book. Furthermore, she kept encouraging me. I will always be thankful for her! I love you, Sweetheart!

Mike Simmons

ACKNOWLEDGEMENTS

I would like to thank those who helped me in this endeavor…

Daniel Todd — Who guided me through the unknown waters of authoring a book.

Leon Martin — Who has been a sounding board for my thoughts and ideas.

J. C. Todd — Who graciously provided editing without laughing too hard at my rookie writing.

Tracey Burgess — Tracey is an old friend who helped me prepare the book for the printer, a task that I found to be far above my skills! Tracey, I owe you!

Pensacola's Finest
CONTENTS

Dedication | *3*

Introduction | *7*

Preface | *10*

The Story Of The Pensacola Police | *15*

The Commanders | *42*

Stories | *70*

Homes Of The Pensacola Police Department | *118*

Spotlights | *125*

Firsts | *138*

End Of Watch | *147*

The Pensacola Police Shield | *174*

Conclusion | *176*

References | *177*

About The Author | *180*

INTRODUCTION

I remember as a child my desire to become a police officer. Not just any police officer, but a Pensacola Police Officer. Maybe it was because my father, Earl James Simmons (Jim to his friends), joined the force when I was two years old, and I wanted to be like him. Like most kids, I played games like *Cops & Robbers*. The difference was that instead of playing *Cowboy & Indians* or *Cops & Robbers*, my siblings — Jackie, Chris, Lisa, Jimmy and I would play The Pensacola Police Department & _____ (whoever the local bad guy was at the time). Mama made me a police uniform and Dad rigged up blue lights on Jimmy's tricycle and my bicycle. Most people don't know what they want to spend their life doing until they are grown, and some never find their niche. But I feel as if I have always known what I wanted to be — a Pensacola Police Officer.

Jimmy and Mike Simmons

Officer Jim Simmons, the author's father

Due to Pensacola Police regulations, I couldn't work for the Department while my dad was there. Consequently, when I reached the age to be employed, I began my career as a Corrections Officer with the Escambia County Sheriff's Department. After my father died in 1982, I joined the force and got to wear his old badge, Number 45. It is difficult to explain the feeling I got when I actually got paid to protect my own neighborhood! It was a great feeling. It sounds strange, but I sometimes felt like Andy Griffith…and I loved it!

During my 30-year career, I worked in many areas of the department, but enjoyed Patrol most. I especially enjoyed working in the downtown area, reminiscing about officers who worked the same streets many years ago. While working in the older downtown area, I became more and more interested in the events that took place during Pensacola's history. I was fascinated to know that, on the exact location that I patrolled, murders were committed, officers pursued suspects, and brother officers died. In 1994, Chief Norman Chapman asked me to add to my portfolio the unofficial and unpaid position of the Department's Historian. I jumped at the opportunity! Soon the task of researching and keeping the historical records was mine (probably because no one else wanted it.)

I found something interesting about writing history — especially history that you have lived with your whole life. In addition to the research involved with finding the details about crimes, criminal, chiefs of police, etc., I also have hundreds of stories told and retold (and probably embellished) over the years. Of course, I can't confirm the validity of all these stories. Some are probably not true, some are not appropriate for this book and others… well, let's just say the statute of limitations hasn't run out yet. But some of the stories help explain how we got to where we are today. Some of them were experienced by me — I lived through them! That is why this is a storybook, not a history book.

I have often thought "what stories from deceased officers in Pensacola's deep history exist? I would like to gather them and keep them." Then I realized that they are gone — buried with the officers. That is the purpose for this book. The stories that I grew up with — that were told to me by my father and other officers who have gone before me — must be preserved. Anyone who gathers with a group of "old-timers" won't be there long before the war stories come out. Like an old comfortable book, the stories are told again and again — usually embellished a little more each time. Old cops are no different. The colorful stories, I have discovered, are like gold. They will never pass this way again. We need to cherish them. Enjoy!

PREFACE

As he was fleeing Florida westward toward the Alabama line, the demons in Ted Bundy took control once again. After a daring escape and an effort to start living a "normal" life in Tallahassee, Ted had murdered two Florida State co-eds and 12-year-old Kimberly Leach. Maybe if he could get away this time, he could start fresh. But it was not to be. The evilness came on him. The monster came out and he had to feed it. He drove into Pensacola and scouted around, looking for his next victim.

The community of Brownsville is located on the west side of town. In the 1970s it was a busy, bustling, middle-class community with mixed business and residential properties. This would work. Ted could find a victim here. He parked his tan Volkswagen Beetle in the parking lot of a busy restaurant — Oscar's — so no one would notice it. Then he got out and scouted on foot. Ted had a unique way of blending in when he wanted and standing out when he needed to. He had done this many times before and had perfected the technique. He would stalk his target while fitting in with the crowd. No one would notice. Then, in an instant, he would turn on the charm. He would solicit a young female and ask for her assistance. Maybe his arm was in a sling, or he was on crutches and needed assistance carrying a bag to his car. Sometimes he portrayed a police officer who needed her to come to the station with him.

Good-looking and charismatic, Ted was also highly intelligent. Not only had he studied law, but he also aspired to be an actor. He had a way of casually approaching women, putting them at ease, and gaining their trust.

But as soon as he got them alone, the monster in him came alive. Much like the story of Dr. Jekyll and Mr. Hyde, his demeanor suddenly changed, and he bludgeoned, stabbed, sexually assaulted, and killed his prey. Then he hid the bodies.

His first known homicides occurred in five northwestern states: Colorado, Washington, Utah, Idaho, and Oregon. His last ones took place in Florida. All in all, he had murdered at least 30 women — but the true number is probably more like 100. Most were sexually assaulted — some he beheaded and kept their heads as a trophy. Some victims have never been found. The scenes of the located victims were often too gruesome to view. Frequently after Ted murdered a victim, he would revisit her hidden grave to relive the event.

The fear created by Ted Bundy in the 1970s paralyzed the country and captivated the attention of the entire world. Then, on February 15, 1978, the killing spree came to an end when he met Pensacola Police Officers David Lee and Norman Chapman. But…maybe part of him did it on purpose.

PENSACOLA'S FINEST:
THE STORY OF THE PENSACOLA POLICE DEPARTMENT

MIKE SIMMONS

THE STORY OF THE PENSACOLA POLICE

Some form of law and order has existed in West Florida as long as people have lived there together. Even the early Pensacola area community of Hawkshaw had rules governing behavior, and punishments that accompanied them. In early times, tribal councils heard cases and dealt punishments which were carried out by the tribal members themselves.

Pensacola's Early Days

On August 15, 1559, Don Tristan de Luna and 1500 people in 11 ships arrived at the charming Pensacola Bay to settle and make the area their home. Included in the population was the *Alcalde Ordinario*, the local law enforcer and judge.[19]

The new settlement didn't last long. On September 19, 1559, a hurricane struck the small community. The residents struggled for two years to survive as a settlement, but without success. Those who remained boarded a ship back to New Spain (Mexico). It wasn't until 1698 that another European settlement was attempted. In 1722, the Spaniards settled on Santa Rosa Island, just east of the site of present-day Fort Pickens[1]. However, when a hurricane suddenly appeared on the horizon, the residents fled to the mainland, near present-day Seville Square.

The British Arrive

In 1763, British troops arrived and took possession of Pensacola. Two months later, the West Florida commission appointed George Johnstone as Captain-General and Governor-in-Chief of West Florida.

On November 27, 1764, members of the British Royal Council appointed themselves and 19 other residents as Justices of the Peace for British West Florida. They appointed John Johnstone as Marshal.

Crime and Punishment

When the British controlled Pensacola, it was a small community with houses mostly near the Bayfront. Shipping was the most important industry, bringing in business from across the world. With the maritime profession came sailors, which created a rowdy waterfront lifestyle. Law & order was important to the citizens of Pensacola. Punishment took on many forms. Besides jail, many creative forms of punishment were used to punish, correct, and deter. Prisoners were often sentenced to be shackled to a pillory in the middle of the town square — today's Ferdinand Plaza.

Pillory

On February 7, 1769, Pensacola council minutes reflect the decision to pay Marshal Johnstone thirty dollars to erect a pillory.[5] Incidentally, neither rain, heat, cold, nor an appeals court had any effect on a judge's sentence. It was the custom that citizens would jeer and throw slimy garbage and rotten eggs at prisoners who were sentenced to endure the pillory. Flogging was also a common punishment. Known as "The Whipping Act of 1530" in England, it was adopted by the British courts in Pensacola. The punishment was carried out when the marshal would tie the prisoner to a vertical pole in the ground by his wrists and beat him. *Tarring & feathering* was also popular. The prisoner would be stripped naked, have hot tar poured or smeared over his body, and feathers thrown on top, so they stuck to the tar — for humiliation. The prisoner was then usually paraded around the town for all to see. This form of punishment often caused permanent injury to the defendant, and occasionally death. One story describes a prisoner who was tarred and feathered, then set on fire and paraded up Palafox Street. William Dunbar, a Pensacola citizen, related the story of one young woman accused of murdering another one; she was convicted and sentenced to have her hand cut off and then to be hanged.[5]

An American Town

Colorful. That is how he was characterized by some. Others used words to describe him: crazy, renegade, and unrefined. He had nicknames such as: "King Mob," "Hero of New Orleans," and "Old Hickory." All of them were accurate to a degree. As a Major General of the Tennessee militia, Andrew Jackson recruited 50,000 volunteers to fight the British in the War of 1812, where he exacted his revenge on the British and became a national hero. He fought the Creek Indians in the Battle of Horseshoe Bend before occupying Pensacola on November 7, 1814. He again invaded Pensacola in 1817, hastening the acquisition of Florida for the United States. He was a common man, a leader of common men, and an enemy to Native Americans. Later, those qualities helped him find his way to the White House.

Two words describe Pensacola in July: hot and humid. Combine that with the other conditions in 1821 — insects, sandy streets, no air conditioning or electric fans and no modern hygiene practices — and it would be difficult to call Pensacola "delightful." The same year, Colonel Don José María Callava was the final Spanish governor of West Florida. Callava had risen through the ranks of the Spanish military rapidly, mostly due to his outstanding war record. He was appointed governor in 1819, before his 40th birthday. As such, he enjoyed supreme power in West Florida. Both Jackson and Callava had some common traits. They both were powerful. Both

Andrew Jackson

were war heroes. Both were egotistical. And both were widely popular within their circles. The two men agreed that Florida would become part of the United States on July 17, 1821 at 10 AM.

On the appointed day, General Jackson rode into town and immediately joined his wife for breakfast. Sharply at 10 AM, amid much ceremony and many American and Spanish soldiers and civilians, the Spanish flag, which had been flying for almost 60 years, was lowered while the Spanish national anthem, *La Marcha Real*, played in Ferdinand Plaza. The plaza was named after Ferdinand VII, the king of Spain. Then, the flag of the United States was proudly raised while the *Star-Spangled Banner* sounded. The ceremony

Plaza Ferdinand

ended with Jackson accepting the territories and the Spanish soldiers boarding their ships and departing. For the first time, the flag of the United States was raised over the territory.[17] Over the next two days, Jackson made appointments to set up the local government. One of the appointments was for James Craig to act as Alguazil, Spanish for constable.

Florida Becomes a State

As his last act as President, John Tyler signed the act into law that gave statehood to Florida. The newly acquired status as a state, the navy yard, and the growing fishing industry caused an increase in the population, as well as the *joie de vivre* of the town. Pensacola was growing, and the town officials knew it was going to take more than one or two men to keep order. Further, the town was quickly becoming a major port, bringing in sailors and visitors from all over the world. Funds were allocated for the hiring of several additional police officers. During this time police officers' mode of travel was by foot. An officer walked to work, to his assigned area, walked while on duty, walked to the stationhouse after his shift, and walked home. Pensacola was growing, and so were the police.

The Civil War Years

The atmosphere in 1860 Pensacola could be described as anxious uncertainty. Or perhaps it was certain — certain war. The impending war between the states was on the minds of everyone. It seemed clear that the only solution to the problem of North vs South was the direction the nation was heading — to fight it out. The arrival of the war brought with it both anxiety and excitement.

On January 10, 1861, Florida seceded from the union. On March 11, 1861, General Braxton Bragg arrived in Pensacola and assumed command of the Confederate troops there. On March 19, eight thousand Confederate soldiers left Pensacola for Tennessee, leaving a skeleton crew to defend the town and nearby installations.

On April 12, our nation officially entered into civil war when Fort Sumter was fired upon. One week later, on April 19, Bragg declared martial law in Pensacola. This meant, in short, that the laws of Pensacola were enforced by members of the Confederate military, not the Pensacola Police. There are no records indicating what services — if any, the civilian police provided, but there is usually action taken to assist the military in such cases.

On May 7, Confederate Colonel Thomas Jones was in charge of the troops in Pensacola. When word came that the formidable Union Admiral David Farragut's fleet was anchored off Mobile Bay, Colonel Jones removed confederate supplies and artillery from Pensacola. On May 9, they set fire to much of the town and left. On the same day, most of the Pensacola citizens abandoned the town, which was surrendered to the Union Forces. City business was conducted from Greenville, Alabama. Less than 100 citizens remained in the vacant town. There is no record of a law enforcement presence in the town during the War. The following day — May 10 — Union Lt. Richard Jackson and his troops moved into and occupied Pensacola. They were warmly greeted by acting mayor John Brosnaham. Northern troops occupied the town and were allowed, unchecked, to roam the town. This left the town in a dilapidated state, with some homes in ashes. Pensacola, initially occupied by Union troops, was eventually completely abandoned.

In 1865, Confederate forces surrendered, ending our nation's worst conflict. Federal troops occupied the Florida capitol city of Tallahassee on May 10. Ten days later, the American flag was again raised over the State Capitol. In Pensacola, citizens began to trickle back into town and try to rebuild the town as well as their lives. However, the military presence remained, which administered most of the law and order in the town until the local government could resume control. On June 25, 1868, the State of Florida and the City of Pensacola were readmitted into the union. The job of rebuilding a nation began.

Uniformed: Pensacola-style
Uniforms had been in existence in Europe for over fifty years, and in larger cities in the United States for thirty years. Even though the idea of policing, patrolling or night watchman duties had been around for hundreds of years, the suggestion of police officers wearing uniforms was just becoming popular across the United States within the last few years. Police uniforms had several advantages. They provided officers with a professional appearance. Citizens could easily identify an officer in time of need. Fellow officers were able to distinguish themselves from suspects and civilians. Uniforms gave the police officers a sense of pride and made them feel like they were part of a crime-fighting army. Arguments for and against wearing them still exist. Officers in uniform are recognizable in times of trouble, but how can they apply a needed low profile in uniform? They bring a sense of comradery to the officers, but do they look "silly?" Regardless, the practice of wearing police uniforms was becoming more accepted,

Pensacola Police Officers, circa 1909

and Pensacola was expected to follow suit. This would be the next step in the rise of professionalism that officers were taking. Besides, many police officers had previously been soldiers and felt comfortable with the military culture. Professional behavior, grooming regulations, camaraderie, and uniforms worked for the military, and many felt it would work well for the police community.

On February 17, 1884, the Pensacola Police Officers donned their first uniforms. "…Pensacola looks more than ever like the city she is. Keep her going!" was the cry from the local newspaper. The uniform, purchased at the officer's expense, consisted of a long navy blue wool coat with two rows of brass buttons and a brass police badge, navy blue wool pants, black leather boots, a black leather belt with a brass buckle, a navy blue police custodian helmet with a hat badge encircled by laurel leaves, and a truncheon (club) which usually hung on the non-club hand side of his belt. If an officer carried a firearm, he had to use his own, but most did.

The new Smith & Wesson Triple Lock .44 revolver was popular, but many officers preferred single action revolvers, or even the repeating pistols used during the Civil War.

In addition, most officers sported a large, heavy duster or handlebar mustache. Suddenly, citizens of Pensacola began to view their officers in a different light. The police became the pride of the city!

An Advance in Technology

Until the early 1880s, if a citizen needed the police or wanted to report something, he went to the police station in person or found an officer walking a beat. So, the entire town was delighted when On March 18, the following article appeared in the *Pensacola Commercial* newspaper: "Resolved, that the committee on public buildings be authorized to place a telephone in the City Marshal's office to facilitate the location of fires, and to render the police more effective." On May 12, 1882, an article in the newspaper *Pensacola Commercial* relayed the editor's opinion of the new contraption:

Telephone Connection

It must be remembered that the city government is connected with the influence of the world by telephone, and therefore all that is necessary, when a fight breaks out or a mob threatens to take possession, is to tap the wires. The city has made this investment with a world view, but candidly speaking, it seems to us as just so much money thrown away.

Reorganization

After the Civil War, the government in Pensacola was ruled by Republicans. Democratic Governor Edward A. Perry, a Pensacolian, urged the Florida legislature to revoke the city charter of Pensacola, which was dissolved on February 16, 1885 and replaced by a provisional government. As a result, the Pensacola Police Department, previously under the command of Marshal Duncan Mallett, was reorganized two days later. Joseph Wilkins, who served as the Escambia County Sheriff (the county where Pensacola is located), was appointed the new City Marshal and Chief of Police.

For the first time, by state constitution, the structure of the police department was spelled out by ordinance. Sixteen officers, under the command of Marshal Wilkins, were now able to keep the city safe more effectively. This new arrangement caused several problems. Because the governor's dissolution of the old form of government and the creation of the new one — controlled by the state, an underlying feeling of resentment by the locals began to grow. But the immediate problem was the appointment of the county's sheriff as marshal. Even though the city commissioners wanted to guide the marshal's movements and directions, he stood as an appointed official — by the governor, not by them. This problem came to a head in the closing weeks of 1886 when Joseph Wilkins was asked — forcefully — to offer his resignation as marshal. He resigned as marshal under protest, but not as sheriff. He then filed a lawsuit to have the case reviewed by the courts. He maintained that the office of Chief of Police should be ruled null and void, because it could not legally usurp the authority of the elected office of Marshal. To replace him, the Board appointed J. B. Roberts as Marshal. At this time, the terms 'marshal' and 'chief of police' began to be used interchangeably because the two titles were almost always held by one man. The difference between the two titles was that the marshal was an elected statutory position while the chief was an appointed employee of the city. Technically, the marshal had no more arrest authority than a rookie police officer.

Mounted Pensacola Police Officer

From 1821 to 1885, law enforcement in Pensacola grew from a one constable to a force of 16 police officers. Now, officers would be on duty all day every day. The first officers were John B. Griffin, Ed Cope, J. G. Gonzalez, Felo Roche, James Farinas, M. C. Gonzalez, John Adams, Mike O'Neal,

A. D. Cromwell, H. Cole, Ed Clark, John Williams, W. R. Gordon, Fransisco Touart and W. R. Kerling. John Griffin was appointed Deputy Marshal and Fransisco Touart was promoted to captain. Monthly pay was:

Marshal Wilkins — $100 (a two-room house cost $300)
Deputy Marshall Griffin — $80 (a 3-year-old steer cost $62)
Captain Touart — $70 (a horse-drawn buggy cost $75)
Officers — $60 (a breech-loading shotgun cost $60)

When the new department was organized, Marshal Wilkins set new rules:
1. Officers could not sit down while on duty.
2. Officers could not drink "spirituous liquor" in the police station.
3. Officers had to be able to read and write in English, never have been indicted and convicted of a crime, of physical health and vigor, of good moral character, and of unquestionable energy.
4. The more intelligent officers were stationed on the main streets.
5. An officer could not use his club or pistol except when he was protecting his life or if someone showed resistance.
6. An officer could not leave his beat unless he was taking an arrestee to the police station or for an emergency.
7. Officers could not visit bar rooms while on or off-duty.
8. An officer could not be absent for roll call more than three times a month.

Tidbits

On April 20, 1885, City Commissioner W.D. Chipley believed that prisoners should be treated better, so he ordered that the ones who worked be allowed three meals a day instead of two, as was the previous norm.

The Department issued each officer one piece of equipment that was effective in the heat, cold, rain, even snow if needed — a whistle.

During the month of December 1885, seventeen prisoners escaped. Fifteen of these were working outside under the guard of one officer, and two of them left from the police station.

Records Section

"Whattyamean I have to write down the guy's name and why I arrested him?" In the late 1800s, officers began to keep track of their arrests and warrants. At first, a log was kept by the officer writing down why he brought each suspect to the station. Once the officers began making "reports," they stored them at the police station in the sergeant's desk. The Police Department then purchased a file cabinet and the Records section was born.

Police Records Section, circa 1960

A change took place when the department moved to 40 South Alcaniz Street in 1956. The Records section grew from a person at a desk with a file cabinet to the new, modern station that included a whole room for keeping records. Record clerks were hired to register criminals, taxis, and dancers.

In 1987, the Department moved to 711 N. Hayne Street, the process of communicating developed into electronic reporting and digital fingerprinting. Clerks no longer needed the massive filing system, freeing up space in the building.

Interesting...

On June 17, 1895, the city commission approved new rules for prisoners:
1. Prisoners after arrest and while in the station house using profane, insulting, or indecent language will immediately be confined to the dungeon and given only bread and water.
2. If a person was fined for an offense but could not pay the fine, he was ordered to work for punishment instead. If he refused to work, he was also placed in the dungeon and fed only bread and water.

The board of public safety was also busy with officer discipline. They handled several suspensions and dismissal hearings every month. In other words, about 20% of the police department changed monthly. Some examples were:

On July 24, 1895, Officer W. H. Ryan came before the Board of Public Safety on the charge of discharging a firearm unnecessarily in the city limits. Ryan pled guilty but stated that he would do it again if he had to. He stated that he shot an escaped prisoner who had been convicted of arson and attempted murder. The case was dismissed.

On October 21, 1895, Officer C. Habberman was dismissed from the Police force for (1) Inefficiency of duty (2) Living with a known prostitute without being married and (3) Obtaining money from a woman and refusing to return it. The officer was dismissed.

In 1896 the Board approved changes in the jail. At the time, female prisoners and male prisoners were housed separately, but under the same roof, and they could still talk to each other. Marshal Wallace ordered a new jail built next door and the female prisoners, described as "irreputable," were housed in the new building.

On April 1, 1896, Marshal Wallace complained to the Board of Public Safety that new, louder whistles were needed, because the current ones could not be heard half a block away. He won his argument and the department received a new, louder whistle for every officer.

On December 1, 1896, Mayor Anderson stated that prisoners who had been allowed to leave the jail at different times, had been found drunk on the streets and had to then be brought back to the station to sober up. This was occurring when the prisoners should have been working. In response, the Board of Public Safety ordered that the following notice be posted in the marshal's office: "No officer shall permit any prisoner to leave or be absent from the prison without a permit from the mayor or the marshal."

If a citizen had an issue with an officer in 1896, he or she would file a complaint with the Board of Public Safety. On December 11, 1896, Mr. John Lear made a complaint against Officer E. C. Briggs for "unwarranted clubbing" him during his arrest. The board of Public Safety investigated the incident and found that the clubbing was justified, and Officer Briggs was found not guilty.

A New Century

With the coming of the 1900s, Pensacola begin to expand and required more police officers. The city commission allocated more funds to hire additional officers. During the next several years, about a dozen new positions were created. As a result, Chief Wilde assigned more officers to the downtown area and some in the newly established neighborhoods such as North Hill and East Hill. During the next 18 years, the police department's budget nearly doubled.

Officers were expected to conduct themselves in a manner befitting their office. The Department began testing officers periodically in their knowledge of the laws and the locations of businesses and streets in their areas. They were also required to be in excellent physical shape to perform their duties. Officers began to work in teams of two, and partners were required to walk the streets for better protection. A local ordinance stated that if two officers were walking down a busy sidewalk and shouted, "Gang Way," people had to move out of their way. Respect or Fear? — probably both.

An advantage offered to officers around the turn of the century was the collection of rewards for capturing wanted persons. For instance, on June 24, 1900, Officer Ward, with the assistance of a citizen, Isau Vau, captured a convicted murderer from Alabama. The sheriff of Lowndes County, Alabama, sent an $8 reward for the deed and it was split between the two.

Tidbits

On June 26, 1901, the City of Pensacola authorized the first plain-clothes officer if it did not cost the city any money. Surveillance and investigations could now by carried out with more efficiency.

In 1895, automobiles became available, and were mass-produced beginning in 1905. However, the police department continued using buggies, horses, and walking. On September 5, 1900, a report was made to the Board of Public Safety that one patrol horse was out of commission due to an injury — it had been kicked by another patrol horse.

Pensacola's Red-Light District

As a town grows, everything grows with it. Businesses grow, infrastructure grows, the economy grows, and criminal activity grows. As the 1900s approached, Pensacola was no exception. Prostitution, the world's oldest profession, was alive and well.

In the late 17th Century, Pensacola was home to the Pacific Fleet, as well as a thriving lumber industry and a booming fishing industry. In addition to the simple growth of the town, the type of businesses attracted prostitutes. Young men with newly earned money were determined to spend it recklessly and abundantly. Many establishments accepted their abundance. The two most popular vices were alcohol

Lady of the Evening

and prostitution. These two evils were not limited to the out-of-town workers. The male citizens — young and old — of Pensacola partook when possible (when mothers and wives weren't looking). Waterfront bars popped up in every space available. While some liquor establishments were legal and proper, many were not. Cheap and dangerous (and sometimes deadly) alcohol was produced and sold to many unsuspecting patrons who were eager to spend their money. The other "evil" brought its own set of problems. In addition to the business being illegal, prostitution was viewed as disease ridden, dirty, and…appealing. In other words, no law was going to stop it. This proved an ever-increasing challenge to the officers. Young men returning from sea or working in the pine forests north of town ventured into the downtown area to find companionship. At the same time, young "coming-of-age" local men and boys were eager to test the waters, often visiting several times a week. Because it was unofficially sanctioned, two unwritten rules applied. First, a concentration of officers on foot patrol were always assigned to the area to respond quickly in case they were needed. Second, officials could arrest the girls or the madam for prostitution or keeping a house of prostitution. It could be said that this was a means of taxing the business.

This profession became so popular that a section of the city was allowed and defined to accommodate it — unofficially. The *Red-Light District* included houses on Zarragossa (called Liberty Street) from Palafox to Barcelona and Baylen from Government to Main Street. The district, known as *The Line*, was a place where sailors and lumbermen frequented without shame, husbands visited secretly, good girls did not go, boys crept in to as much as possible, and, if a wife was seen there, someone was in trouble. Extra police patrols were assigned to the area, which was informally allowed to operate — if two requirements were met. First, the girls had to be disease free to conduct business. Second, if the police were in search of a law breaker, the girls had to inform them of his whereabouts.

The bordellos ranged from run-down and dirty to clean and elegant, with a feel of classy. Some of the houses in the area were very nice. A few of the madams had nicely decorated rooms, which they kept clean and appealing. This ambiance helped attract wealthy clients.

The types of girls available also varied. They ranged from elegantly dressed girls who refused to undress with the light on to those who would yell and flash men from the street corner. Many of the madams would not allow their girls to drink or smoke while "on duty." The idea was to give the look of a good American girl to the customers. Others didn't care how they lured the men, as long as they made money. The customers got what they paid for.

The most famous Pensacola madam was Mollie McCoy, who operated a house at 15 W. Liberty Street. In a September 5, 1982 edition of the *Pensacola News Journal*, Dot Brown wrote an article entitled "The History that Almost Made Pensacola Famous." In the article, she quoted from Danton Walker's biography, "Standing under the hall light was the madam herself, a large, stout woman of about 60, dressed in black lace. Her hair, in a weird shade of pink, was worn in a high pompadour and her face was heavily rouged. Her puffy hands sparkled with small diamond rings." Almost as much as she was at her brothel, Mollie found herself in court — being charged, paying a fine, or being sentenced jail. Mollie died at the age of 78 and was buried in St. John's cemetery. It is a local legend among young men that, if they make their way to Mollie's grave and rub her headstone, they will have luck with the ladies that night.

Brothel of Molly McCoy
15 W. Zarragossa St.

World War I brought about a temporary end to the bordellos, since the U.S. government requested that they be closed. After the war, the businesses reopened, but were shut down — this time for good — during WWII. Maybe not stopped, but prostitution was not allowed to be conducted in the open.

After the war ended, even though the practice of prostitution didn't stop, bordellos became less practical, partly due to the popularity of automobiles. Street-corner prostitutes became more common. Also, the romance of bordellos was replaced with girls that swap sex for money to get drugs. Robbery and theft accompanied the new generation of prostitutes.

Girls plied their trade on south Palafox Street until the waterfront commerce began to slow. The girls still needed a home base; therefore, in the late 1970s, the old Hotel San Carlos at Palafox and Garden Streets became popular for prostitution shopping. The business also moved to the old motels along west Cervantes Street and Mobile Highway. In 1993, the San Carlos was demolished, so the go-to thriving shopping mall for prostitutes scattered throughout town. The bottom line — prostitution has been around for a long time, and it's not leaving any time soon!

Pensacola Police Communications

The city bell. Everyone had heard it, and everyone knew what its function was. A large, 3000 lb. bell at the police station was rung on special occasions, for celebrations, and when needed to communicate, such as a fire or other emergency. Officers were required to know the following:

> *One bell from the tower means that the Captain of the Watch is wanted. Two bells the mounted officer is wanted. It is his duty to go to the nearest telephone and call up the station; if no phone is handy, he must go to the station at once and report.*
>
> *Three bells mean that all the officers ON and OFF duty MUST report at the police headquarters AT ONCE. (NO EXCUSE WILL BE TAKEN FROM ANY OFFICER FOR FAILING TO REPORT TO THIS CALL.)*

It was a welcomed change when, on May 17, 1909, telephones were first installed in the police station followed by call boxes positioned at street corners around the city. From these call boxes, officers could call the police station, maintaining and coordinating their activities. It became department policy for officers to call in periodically and check for calls on their beat. However, if there was an emergency, the desk sergeant still rang the city bell, but the rules changed. For instance, if the officer was working Beat 3, the desk sergeant would ring the bell three times indicating him to call the station. The boxes remained in place until the early 1980s. For an officer to make a call on a police box he was given the following directions:

> "Open the outside and inside door of the box. Strike six blows with your finger on the gutla percha in the lower corner of the box. Then push in the gutla percha pin in the upper corner of the box, count to fifty (50) and then pull the lever."

Oddly enough, officers found this new method of communication to be effective. The boxes were located strategically around the city so that there was always one close by if needed. The following are some of the locations:

Pensacola Wharf	Government & Palafox
Government & Baylen	Baylen & Zarragossa
Government & "C"	Government & Devilliers
Garden & Devilliers	Tarragona & Zarragossa
Government & Fla Blanca	Romana & Tarragona
Intendencia & Cevallos	Intendencia & 10th Ave
L&N Railroad Wharf	Barcelona & Gregory
Wright & Devilliers	LaRua & Reus
Spring & Gadsden	Jackson & Palafox
LaRua & "C"	Palafox & Desoto
Tarragona & Chase	Cevallos & Wright
Gregory & 10th Ave	Tarragona & Wright
Gadsden & Alcaniz	Gadsden & Cevallos
L&N Freight Depot	L&N Roundhouse
Desoto & Alcaniz	Muscogee Wharf

Less than a month later, a new police call box was used to report one of the department's own. On June 10, 1909 Officer Joseph G. Hilliard, who was off duty, visited *The Alligator*, a bar located at Wright and Tarragona streets for a drink. While there, his pistol dropped from his pocket onto the ground. Seeing his intoxicated condition, the employees asked him to leave, and they later filed a complaint at the police house. Meanwhile, Hilliard proceeded to another bar at the corner of Tarragona and Garden streets and began cursing and acting disorderly toward a man named Joe Morris. The police were called, and Officer W. M. Malone was dispatched to the bar using the new call boxes. When Officer Malone arrived, he refused to arrest a fellow officer. The behavior of both officers brought them reprimands.

Even though the radio, known as a "wireless," had been around for some time, new developments occurred in 1913. Woodrow Wilson gave the first presidential press conference via radio on March 14, 1913. Over the next several years, the worth of the new technology of radio was realized. The use of radio for naval vessels, music, news, and long-distance communication came into play across the world. Soon, police departments began to experiment with the use of one-way radios for dispatching patrol cars and for the dissemination of information. Finally, the technology came to Pensacola. On Thursday, April 23, 1925, the Pensacola Journal reported the following:"Council instructed city manager Roark to advertise for bids for purchase of a police radio short wave set. Council was told that the Radio Corporation of America has already offered to the city a radio set for $2320, and which would require only $200 a year to operate." After delays and budget constraints, the system was finally installed in all patrol cars. The base system was installed in the desk sergeant's office at the police station.

Old Police Radio

The 1939 P280 desktop two-way radio monitor operated a base station (not shown), allowing communications between dispatchers at police headquarters and radio-equipped police cars.

For the previous 60 years, the city bell had been used to dispatch. However, after the installation of the radio system, the bell had to be taken out of use. According to the January 2, 1936 edition of the *Pensacola News Journal*, "It was the only time since the construction of the jail building that the desk sergeant and turn-key on watch at the time have not swung the bell rope lustily by way of celebrating the new year." The first transmissions of the radio system from the station to the patrol cars occurred on January 4, 1936. The content is not known. The Pensacola Police Department dispatcher was born!

Unfortunately, the radios in the cars could not transmit — only receive. The desk sergeant put out calls to a patrol car three times in the hope that the officer heard at least one. It didn't take long for the radio system to be put to the test. A few hours after the radio was tested, a call was put out to Officer Clinton Green, dispatching him to respond to the Piggly Wiggly on Palafox Street to apprehend two shoplifters. Three minutes later they were in custody. Pensacola was proud of her new purchase.

On August 9, Chief O'Connell announced that the city would be receiving bids for new two-way police radios to be installed in all police cars. Using this new technology, officers could communicate back and forth with the desk sergeant directly.

When the Pensacola Police Department moved to the new location at 40 South Alcaniz Street in 1956, dispatching was considered. However, a dispatch section was not provided for. Modern times called for a separate dispatch section. The desk sergeant had doubled as a dispatcher. Now, however, a room was set aside for dispatchers. Officers had two-way radios where they could communicate with dispatchers, but not with each other. The two-person dispatch room was approximately 6'x 6'. Dispatchers from that era

The Motorola Police Cruiser one-way radio was designed to receive broadcasts in police cars. This 1936 ad showed (left to right) the radio receiver, speaker and controls.

tell the story that, to get in or out of the room, one was required to climb over the other. Later, dispatchers moved to a much larger room — 8'x 12'. Today, it is difficult to over-emphasize the importance of the Pensacola Police Communications Center. It is the very nerve center of the entire department. Officers speak to telecommunicators more often than any other employees. It is vital to the police function in Pensacola.

On February 19, 2019, in an interview with retired Supervisor Dixie Chancellor about the Communications section, she related the following:

> *"When I first started (in 1973), the dispatch center consisted of two chairs in a room approximately 8' by 12' with a microphone to push and talk to the officers. I cannot remember how many channels other than Patrol, Investigations, possibly a mutual aid, and one for the Gulf Breeze Police Department. Also had possibly 4 phone lines and ring down lines to the Sheriff's Office and Pensacola Fire Dept. There was not a 911 system during this time. When we moved from 40 S. Alcaniz St to 711 N. Hayne St in 1987, things began to change to the more modern Communications Center of today. The Fire dispatchers joined us, and we became the main dispatch center for Public Safety in the City limits. It took several years before our first CAD (computer aided dispatch) system was added, and we became a Public Safety Answer Point for the Escambia 911 system."*

Civil Unrest of the 1960s

In the 1960s, the issue of civil rights was THE issue. The problem is as old as our country. Thomas Jefferson, the primary author of the United States' Declaration of Independence, wrote, "We hold these Truths to be self-evident, that *all Men are created equal*, that they are endowed by their Creator with certain unalienable Rights, that among these are Life, Liberty, and the Pursuit of Happiness...." However, all men were not treated as equals. White males ruled our country. Even though slavery had been around

Pensacola Police riot control training in the 1960s

for many centuries and had been the norm, more people began to voice their opinions that it was wrong, and the problem, along with other issues, brought our country to war with ourselves. After slavery was abolished, the next challenge was even more difficult — to make changes so that everyone is afforded equal treatment under the law.

However, in the 1960s, the acceptance of written and previously accepted laws defying our country's stated words of independence were challenged. The courage of Dr. Martin Luther King, Rosa Parks and others paved the way for peaceful demonstrations that eventually made significant changes.

But, as with any new development, problems followed. While most civil demonstrations were peaceful across the country, horrible violence broke out in pockets. In communities across the United States, especially in Philadelphia, Harlem and Rochester, riots were often planned and well-organized. In most places, however, rioting was either a violent spinoff of a peaceful demonstration, or impulsive actions stemming from an incident. In Pensacola, riots were limited to a few areas of town. On August 30, 1969, 20 arrests — mostly young men — were made at the intersection of Belmont and DeVilliers Streets. The charges came from incidents including resisting arrest, drunkenness, loitering, or failure to obey a lawful order.

A year later, the first weekend of August 1970 brought a wave of unbridled trouble to the city. Throughout the city, the Pensacola Police had their hands full. Forty young people connected to riot-related incidents were arrested, while several citizens went to the hospital and numerous police officers were injured by thrown rocks, bottles, and Molotov cocktails. One young man with a shotgun was stopped by an off-duty police officer, who was found with four shotgun shells in his pocket.

Lineup – 1972

Reported were three firearms discharged, seven assaults (two requiring hospital treatment), 15 cases of vandalism, 16 cases of arson and attempted arson, as well as a variety of related burglary and theft charges. In addition to the police trouble, the Pensacola Fire Department responded to 19 riot-related fires.

Almost as quickly as they started, the problems stopped. Despite the violent criminal action, progress toward equal treatment was made. There is still work to be done in all areas, and folks will never be perfect as long as they are human.

The Police Profession becomes more…Professional

Pensacola Police Officers circa 1959

One problem that the world of law enforcement suffered from was a lack of training. Chief Caldwell realized the occupation of police officer was no longer simply a job. More and more often it was viewed as a profession. Therefore, it was necessary to initiate formal training for officers. In an interview with Chief Caldwell, he stated that he helped design a new school in which students were required to attend and graduate from to become a police officer. Consequently, the beginnings of the Florida police academy were established. Later, Chief Davis was key in the expansion of the police academy to become an established institution in the police profession throughout the state. Today, every law enforcement officer in Florida is required to complete state-regulated training, pass a state exam, a polygraph, and a psychological exam before being certified as an officer.

Pensacola's Abortion Issues

1984 — Four abortion clinic bombings literally shook Pensacola. No one was injured, but a lot of property was damaged. One bombing took place in the summer and three in the early morning hours on Christmas morning. Two of the bombings occurred within the city limits and were investigated by the Pensacola Police Department. Pipe bombs were used in all four. It appeared that all incidents were related. Working with the Pensacola Police detectives were investigators from the Escambia County Sheriff's Department and the U. S. Bureau of Alcohol, Tobacco and Firearms. From the physical evidence, the detectives identified and arrested four suspects: James Simmons - 20, Matt Goldsby - 20, Kay Wiggins - 18, and Kathren Simmons - 19. Because of the BATF's involvement, the suspects were charged in federal court. Defense attorneys argued that the young people bombed the clinics to save babies. After a trial that got nationwide attention, all four defendants were convicted. While the ladies received probation, the men were sentenced to 10 years in federal prison.

March 10, 1993 — Just prior to 10 AM, Michael Griffin, armed with a .38 caliber revolver, entered the rear of the Women's Medical Service abortion clinic located at Cordova Square, 12th Avenue and Bayou Blvd. In the rear of the building, Griffin approached Dr. David Gunn, 47, and shot him three times at point-blank range. Dr. Gunn was transported to nearby

Sacred Heart Hospital but died a short time later. On the same day, Griffin turned himself into Pensacola Police Officers. On March 5, 1994, Griffin was found guilty and sentenced to life in prison.

116 days later, on July 29, 1994 — Paul Hill, a former minister, who often protested against abortion providers, got out of his vehicle at *The Ladies Center*, 6770 N. 9th Avenue. He was armed with a 12-gauge shotgun. At 7:30 AM, he approached abortion doctor John Britton and his driver James Barrett and shot both in the head, killing both men immediately. He also wounded Mr. Barrett's wife, June. Mr. Hill waited for the police officers to arrive and gave up. Mr. Hill never denied his actions. He was convicted of first-degree murder in December 1994 and given the death penalty. As his date for the death penalty arrived, Hill refused to file an appeal, stating that he was ready to die. Hill was executed in 2003.

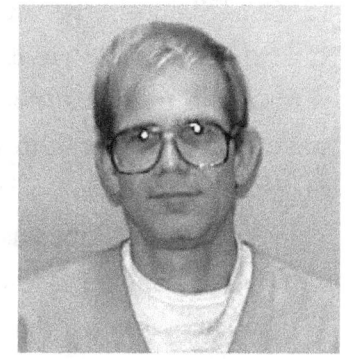
Paul Hill

Pensacola's Storms — Hurricanes

Police officers in every state, county, city, and town know that, when a person signs up for the job, it is not relegated to 8–5 Monday thru Friday. Shift work, bad accidents, hostage standoffs, and natural emergencies — can appear at any moment.

For those officers in the United States who work along the coast, the days between June 1 and November 30 are always considered when trying to schedule a vacation. Those days mark hurricane season — when every day begins by looking at the weather report to see what is looming off the coast. According to the severity of the storm, officers might have to work late, overnight, or for several days. They are the first into a problem and the last out. And it is a pretty sure bet that, in Pensacola, every season will bring at least a few days of hurricane duty. Since the Europeans first settled here and began keeping records, hurricanes have paid frequent visits, and each one has brought unique challenges for Pensacola's finest.

The hurricane of 1559 began Pensacola's recorded relationship with tropical storms. Besides the 1559 hurricane, Pensacola was struck in 1693, 1715, 1722 and 1742. During the British period, three storms were reported — 1766, 1772 and 1778. The people of the town experienced injury, damage, and expense. After Pensacola became part of the United States, a hurricane is reported to have struck in September 1825. The governor and mayor stated that the parts of town near the water had been devastated by storm surge. After the U.S. War Between the States ended, another storm struck. This one was described as causing moderate damage, but not widespread, with minor damage to homes.

Pensacola experienced another severe hurricane in 1896. The storm damaged homes, warehouses, roads, and railroad tracks, but no lives were lost. This brought about the establishment of the National Weather Service. After 1896, major hurricanes struck Pensacola in 1906, 1916, 1926 and 1936. Records indicate that great damage was done to homes, storage facilities, ships, the new aircraft at the Pensacola Naval Air Station, Railroad tracks, and power lines. Hurricanes also struck in 1947, 1953, 1979, 1985, 1995(2), 2004 and 2005. In every case, Pensacola Police Officers have had to work long and tiring hours to serve the citizens.

The most expensive Pensacola hurricane as of this writing was Hurricane Ivan which made landfall on September 16, 2004, made landfall as a Category 3 with sustained winds of 145 mph. Just before landfall, the Pensacola Police Department went into emergency mode. Half the department was placed on day shift and half on night shift. Officers assisted citizens with evacuations from homes and businesses, as well as helping them to shelters. Other officers were assigned to the shelters. When the storm hit, many people who had refused to evacuate before now called 911 in an effort for someone to rescue them. After the winds reached hurricane strength, the order was passed for all officers to get off the streets and find shelter for the duration of the storm. Afterwards, the National Guard was called out to assist.

After the storm passed, the shock of the damage ensued. In some cases, entire homes were missing, and others were severely damaged. The infrastructure (electricity, water, sewerage, etc.) was out, and it took several weeks to repair it in some cases. People were not prepared for the damage that was done. Not only did Pensacola Police officers have to work through the storm, initial shock, damage assessment, and cleanup, but they were not allowed to work on their own homes. However, in times of despair, the best often comes out in people. Family, friends, neighbors, and fellow officers worked on officers' homes, bringing them to a livable level. Officers patrolled for looting, directed traffic, and simple maintained order in a city with no structure. They also rescued people who were trapped, delivered ice, and did what was necessary to bring the city back to where it once was. Pensacola never completely returned to the way it was before Ivan's visit, but it did recover — thanks in part to the police officers of Pensacola.

THE COMMANDERS

Throughout Pensacola's rich history, many officers have been named to take the lead in keeping law and order. Over the years, some records have been lost or destroyed, making a comprehensive list of department heads difficult, and maybe impossible. Below is a list beginning with the arrival of the British government in 1763:

Provost Marshal and Deputy Provost Marshal: Under British rule in West Florida (1763–1781), a Provost marshal oversaw the law enforcement for the entire territory — East and West Florida. The marshal overseeing the law enforcement in Pensacola was officially called the "Deputy Provost Marshal." However, known as the "Marshal," he was the final law enforcement authority in town. He was the head of the local police. An addition was enacted on July 30, 1771 when the "Establishing the Method of Appointing Constables" act was passed. As progress was made in British West Florida, the need for local officers became more apparent. In response, the British government created the 1771 act for constables to act under the authority of the Deputy Provost Marshal. Constables were far from the trained professional law enforcement officers of the 21st century. Every man 21–55 was mandated to serve his term in the office. The new mandate revealed that both the British government and the local fathers needed more for law enforcement than was previously thought.

- **James Johnstone, Marshal: November 1, 1764–August 24, 1766**
  In 1764, shortly after Great Britain acquired West Florida from Spain, the British Provincial Council appointed one man to hold the positions of deputy provost marshal and marshal of the territory — James Johnstone.

Even though these two positions held specific duties, they were performed together by one person — the nephew of the governor.

If one traveled from Great Britain to Pensacola in May, a huge surprise awaits, as visitors arrived on the shores of the northern gulf coast in May. Pensacola natives often witnessed the shedding of coats and hats. The British were not accustomed to the high temperature and humidity of Florida. When Marshal Johnstone stepped off the ship on May 8, 1765, he no doubt felt the change immediately. Historical documents infer that Marshal Johnstone was less than pleased with his appointed station, and the hot and muggy weather likely contributed to his unhappiness.

One of the first recorded arrests made in West Florida occurred in 1766[4]. Governor Johnstone already has a reputation as a controversial leader and often found himself at odds with the military leaders in Pensacola. On one occasion, the governor and British Lieutenant Colonel Ralph Walsh, a newcomer to the area, had a disagreement of the disposal of government property. Johnstone ordered the arrest of Walsh by military officials. The order fell on the shoulders of Walsh's contemporary, Lieutenant Colonel Edward Maxwell, who refused to carry it out, despite the governor's insistence. Exasperated, Johnstone ordered his nephew to arrest Walsh. When that didn't work, the governor himself arrested Walsh and turned him over to his nephew. Within days, Walsh was released and ordered to Mobile, Alabama against the governor's wishes.[7]

- **John Sammay, Marshal: August 24, 1766–January 1, 1767**
- **John Crozer, Marshal: May 24, 1769**
- **Alexander McCullagh, Marshal: 1772–June 24, 1776** — Marshal McCullagh was paid 30 pounds per year to serve as gaol (jail) keeper. His other duties included tracking, apprehending, and maintaining custody of state prisoners. He remained marshal until the Spaniards took control of the Floridas in 1781.
- **James Craig, Alguazil:1821**

Upon accepting his new territory, Governor Andrew Jackson got to work setting up the government of the new town of Pensacola. On July 18 and 19, he appointed officials to preside over the local government. For the position of *alcalde*, he named his longtime friend, Judge Henry Brackenridge. The *alcalde* was an all-powerful position, second to the governor. Other appointments included: George Bowie, *Mayor*, William Bennett, Henry Michelet, John Innerarity, and John Brosnaham, *Aldermen*. Dr. Bronough became *resident physician*, John D. Vooerhees was named *Health Officer*, and Oliver Clark was appointed *Harbor Master*. On the 19th, he also appointed James Craig as the *alguazil*, which is the Spanish word for Constable, Marshal and Police Officer[18].

On October 11, 1823, the *Pensacola Gazette* published a new ordinance describing the duties of the city constable:

An Ordinance for the City of Pensacola

Sec 2d: There shall be appointed by the Mayor a person to be called the City Constable, and another person who shall be recommended by the City Constable, and for whose acts he shall be responsible, to act as his deputy.

Sec 3d: It shall be the duty of the City Constable and his deputy, to see that all Ordinances of the Board of Aldermen are duly executed, and to cite and bring before the Mayor all offenders, in order that they may be duly proceeded against. — It shall also be their express duty to arrest and confine, until they can be brought before the Mayor, for examination, all disorderly and suspicious persons and slaves found abroad without written permission from their masters or mistresses, after the ringing of the Bell, which it shall be the duty of the City Constable to cause to be rung at eight P. M. from 15th September to 15th April, and at nine P. M. from 15th April to 15th September in each year.

- **J. N. Brown, Constable: 1822–1823**
- **James Ingraham, Constable: 1823–1824**

- **Fransisco Comyns, Constable: 1824–1825**
- **Foster Chapman, Constable: 1825–1827**
- **Fransisco Comyns, Constable: 1827–1830**
- **Henry Nunes, Constable: 1830–1830**

City Marshal: With the number of sailors, civilian workers and family members slowly increasing, law enforcement in began adjusting keep up with the demand. As expectations rose, so did the number of employees, the amount of equipment, and the need for a new jail. When the United States Navy made a home in Pensacola, the city fathers quickly realized that the current system in place for enforcing the laws was insufficient and needed improving. They researched the latest practices in law enforcement in the United States.

In old France, some of the great homes were so large and complex that they employed a stable officer known as a *mareschal*. Before long, this term came to refer to the officer of the house. The title became so lauded that the English translation, Marshal, began to be used for the head officer of armies and countries. Across the sea, the title was often used as the head of law enforcement, and the town of Pensacola was no exception.

- **Edward Senae, City Marshal: 1830–1834**
  On June 12, 1830, Pensacola's first elected City Marshal, Edward Senae, took control of the law enforcement in the town.

- **John Gonzalez, City Marshal: 1834–1837**
- **Elliott Headington, City Marshal: 1836–1838**
- **John Stuckey, Jailor: 1837**
- **Peter Woodbine, Jailor: 1839**
- **George Willis, City Marshal: 1838–1844**

- **Lafayette Robertson, Jailor: 1843**
- **Frances Touart, City Marshal: 1844–1846**
- **Fransisco Comyns, Constable: 1877**
- **George Wells, City Marshal: 1882–1883**
- **Richard Gagnet, City Marshal: 1883–1885**
- **Duncan Mallett, City Marshal: January 1885–February 1885**
- **Joseph Wilkins, City Marshal: February 1885–March 1885**
- **Duncan Mallett, City Marshal: March 1885–January 1887**

- **J. B. Roberts, City Marshal & Chief of Police: January 1, 1887–January 15, 1889**

    As Marshal Wilkins resigned, the city commissioners, with the governor's approval, appointed J. B. Roberts as Marshal. He also became the chief of police. However, it was soon realized that, per ordinance, the chief of police must be a Pensacola Police Officer, which Roberts was not. Consequently, J. B. Roberts resigned, recommending Captain Connors to replace him.

- **William H. Connors, Chief of Police: April 26, 1889–March 8, 1891**

On February 14, 1890, the following article appeared in the *Daily News*: "By the provisions of the law creating the municipality of Pensacola, the Sheriff of the county is made marshal of the city and head of the police force. All recommendations for appointment on the force are made by him for the Police Committee of the City Board. The Chief of Police has the immediate supervision of the force when on duty."

W. H. Connors, Chief of Police

In 1885, *The Pensacola News* reported on a lawsuit brought about by Joseph Wilkins, who had been stripped of his *City Marshal* position. On March 8, 1891, *The Pensacola News* reported that the lower trial court and the state court of appeals had ruled against Wilkins, but the State Supreme Court ruled in his favor, giving him back the office of marshal.

- **Joseph Wilkins, City Marshal: March 8, 1891–August 22, 1893**
  After Joseph Wilkins was reinstated as marshal in 1891, he held the office respectfully. He did not seek reelection for marshal in August 1893. On October 29, 1893, Joseph Wilkins, while in the community of Millview west of town, died suddenly. The funeral took place at St. Michael's church on Palafox Street at 10:30 AM on October 31. It was said to be one of the largest funerals Pensacola has ever seen. His remains were brought from Millview to the home of James, his brother, on Intendencia Street. From there a procession of many people made their way to Palafox Street and up to the church. After the funeral, the burial took place at St. Michael's cemetery.

- **William H. McDavid, City Marshal: August 22, 1893–June 7, 1895**
  As the election for marshal inched closer, six officers threw their names in the race for the position. William McDavid and James Farinas, officers with the department, received the most votes. Captain McDavid received 213 votes and Captain Farinas received 127. On August 22, 1893, William McDavid assumed the office of marshal. He held the office capably until the time for his reelection on June 7, 1895. He decided to run again, against the popular train conductor, Edward Wallace. The race was a tight one, and well-publicized. On June 4, Marshal McDavid withdrew his name, allowing Mr. Wallace an easy victory.

- **Edward A. Wallace, City Marshal: June 7, 1895**
  On Friday June 7, 1895, Edward A. Wallace was elected as town marshal. He had already accepted the position of chief of police. By 1899 Wallace had gone to work for the railroad. On July 2, 1900 at the age of 39-years old he was involved in a railroad accident near Selma, Alabama in a small town called Aldrich. He was a conductor on the Southern Railway run between Selma and

Birmingham when he lost his footing and fell beneath the train and was killed. His wife's brother, Fred Massy, took the responsibility to go to his Warrington home and inform his wife of her husband's death. His body was returned to Pensacola and buried in St. Michael's Cemetery.

- **Frank Wilde, City Marshal & Chief of Police: December 31, 1897–June 4, 1901**

On December 31, 1897, Frank Wilde was elected the new Pensacola *Marshal*. It was not until 1931 that the city officials reorganized the form of government and began operating under a city manager that the chief became the department head with full authority over his agency. At that time, they dissolved the position of marshal and the police department head was simply the chief. Wilde was initially appointed by the Board as Deputy City Marshal. However, it was determined that, because Mr. Wilde was not a police officer, he was ineligible to hold the office of deputy city marshal. So, on July 16, 1897 the Board appointed him policeman on the reserve list, and on July 23, he was elected by unanimous vote of the board members as deputy city marshal. Marshal Wilde immediately began recruiting officers based on their toughness, both mentally and physically, to keep law and order in this growing and spirited town.

- **Ammie A. Credille, City Marshal & Chief of Police: June 4, 1901–June 4, 1903**

On June 4, 1901, Frank Wilde and Ammie A. Credille competed in the election for marshal in which Credille won. Wilde continued as a captain on the force. Frank Wilde died on July 8, 1932 after a short illness at the age of 76 years. He is buried in St. John's Cemetery.

An interesting fact about Marshal Credille: Not long after he was hired on July 14, 1899, he was brought up on internal charges by Marshal Frank Wilde for simply talking to a private citizen, which violated a police department rule. He plead not guilty but was convicted and suspended for 30 days. The next July 28, a relative, RA Credille, testified that the officer had been under great stress from all the sickness in his family. He was exonerated.

- **C. F. Schad, City Marshal and Chief of Police: June 4, 1903– October 31, 1906**
Marshal C. F. Schad took over a department that suffered from corruption and low morale. However, he built up spirits and reputation day by day, simply by doing his job.

Was it a conflict of interest? Marshal C. F. Schad had to ask himself. After all, it was a reasonable question. The marshal had been wrestling with the offer of partnering with Allie Riera to open a saloon. He had just gone through the act of commanding the police force through a major hurricane, and he felt that he needed to make a decision. He sought the advice of numerous people about the wisdom of the marshal embarking on the new venture, which paid more than his marshal's salary. When no one could sufficiently advise him, he decided for himself, and resigned to Mayor Bliss. On October 31, 1906, his last day as Marshal, his successor, Milton Frank, and Captain Fondebilla presented him with a silk umbrella at a banquet held in his honor.

In 1944, long after his retirement, Fred Schad made a trip to New Orleans for an operation. Because of the perils of the trip and operation, he developed pneumonia and died. His body was returned to Pensacola and buried in St. John's Cemetery.

- **Milton Frank, City Marshal and Chief of Police: October 31, 1906– June 5, 1907**
The morning after honoring Marshal Schad, Milton Frank began his new job as marshal. He held the position until a new marshal was elected in 1907. As elections go, the prospects for regular election for marshal proved to be a heated one in 1907. Milton Frank, the current

marshal, was a candidate, along with Captain Fondebilla, Deputy Sheriff Frank Sanders, and others. Each man had a tough job to do while campaigning heavily. Further, Frank and Fondebilla were not keen on Sanders, the only candidate from the sheriff's office. Candidates ran on integrity, frugal spending, and experience. It was a tough race, but Sanders prevailed.

Interesting facts about Milton Frank. The Frank family lived at 418 South "E" Street, on the corner of Main street. In July of 1912, his daughter, Anna Bell, who was four years-old, became ill and died a few days later, on July 11. Her burial took place in St. Michael's cemetery. Four months later, on November 11, 1912, Frank filed a request in court for a restraining order to stop the *Gulf, Florida, and Alabama Railroad* from running a track on his property. Apparently, the railroad company had begun surveying and excavating to lay track along the north side of Main street — on his property — without his permission. After a court battle, Frank won. The tracks were laid on the south side of the road.

In 1918, Milton Frank had worked his way to the rank of Police Captain. The Frank family home was situated only a few blocks from Pensacola Bay. June 11, 1918 was a typical hot day in Pensacola. Three of Milton Frank's daughters, 18-year-old Ruth, 14-year-old Hilda, and 12-year-old Nellie went for a cool dip in the bay, along with their brother-in-law, Joe Russell. None of the girls could swim, but the bay was shallow and was only a few feet deep. Unknown to the girls, dredging had recently taken place in that area. All three girls went under at the same time. Joe rescued the younger girl, Nellie, but could not find the other girls once he returned. One body was pulled from the bay at 10 PM and the other at 1 am. Page 6 of the *Pensacola Journal* contained an article entitled "Double Funeral of Two Unfortunate Sisters at 4:30 P. M." that started like this: "Two white-clad bodies, the embodiment of purity which was theirs in life, and thus emphasized in death, lay at the home of Captain and Mrs. Milton B. Frank last night, and a room scented with the choicest of flowers, was crowded with friends, for the terrible tragedy of the night before was learned of with most sincere grief when *Journal* readers picked up their morning paper early yesterday."

- **Frank D. Sanders, City Marshal & Chief of Police: June 6, 1907– November 7, 1916**
Frank Dent Sanders walked into his new office. He had his work cut out for him. As an outsider, he now commanded the police department, and his priority was reorganization. To keep down mutinous thoughts and actions from the insiders that he defeated for the position, he demoted Captain Fondebilla to patrolman and Marshal Frank to turnkey. Of course, these arrangements were disputed, and the case was taken to the Board of Public Safety, who approved the new Marshal's actions.

Frank Sanders was born on August 26, 1867, in Barbour County, Alabama and arrived in Pensacola in 1893. He married Ida Anastasia Duval Christie on September 4, 1899, in Pensacola's St. Joseph's Church. They had nine children, all born in Pensacola. His first job was as chief deputy under Sheriff George Smith, his brother in law. Sheriff Smith was quite ill at the time and relinquished almost all the duties of his office to Sanders. It was from this position that he became well-known as a good officer and a leader with a level head. As a result, he won the election of marshal in 1908.

Upon taking over, Chief Sanders immediately realized that the 12-hour shift for five to seven days a week was too much for his fellow officers. In addition to the lack of family time, the excessive hours greatly reduced the department's efficiency. As a result, Chief Sanders instituted a standard 8-hour shift, three shifts per twenty-four-hour period. This shift remained in effect until the 1980s.

Among the many issues that Marshal Sanders encountered was that of discipline. Officers sometimes conducted themselves in a manner unbefitting their position. For example, Marshal Sanders had to decide what to do about the actions of Officer Burrel Lowry when, on July 28, 1908, he emptied his revolver at a fleeing suspect near Union Depot after an attempted arrest. His negligence forced the Marshal to charge Lowery with reckless shooting and forward his case to the Board of Public Safety. The Board heard the case and suspended the officer for a period of 24-hours with a reprimand placed in his file. During his law enforcement career, Officer Lowry developed a reputation for provocation in most of his dealings, causing more than one internal investigation. On August 9, 1915, James Harrison shot at his brother-in-law Benjamin "Tom" Majors at Harrison's home. After several shots were fired at him, Majors returned fire, mortally wounding Harrison. A coroner's jury convened and, after hearing the evidence, cleared Majors of any wrongdoing. However, Officer Lowry improperly inserted himself and his influence into the case and had to once again be reprimanded. In 1916, Lowry separated from police service and became a shipyard worker.

Frank Sanders…Most Popular Person in The City: On November 7, 1916, Chief Sanders lost his bid for sheriff of Escambia county. Meanwhile, the city commissioners eliminated the chief of police position, leaving the duties of running the department up to the commissioner of police. On June 11, 1917, Sanders was elected to the office of city commissioner, was re-elected in June of 1920 and again in June of 1923. He served at different times as mayor, commissioner of finance and revenue, commissioner of streets and public works, and finally the police and fire commissioner, which he held until his death. Prior to his election to the office of city commissioner, Sanders served the city as special police officer, deputy marshal, city marshal, and chief of police. He died in 1925 at the age of 58 and his funeral was held in his home on Wednesday, November 18, 1925. The *Pensacola News Journal* reported that Frank Sanders was "the most popular person in the city."

- **Cary Ellis, Chief of Police: June 10, 1918–December 31, 1920**

  In 1891, a 17-year-old named Cary Ellis from Alabama began his career with the L & N Railroad in Pensacola as a newsboy. After only a year, Ellis was promoted to Brakeman, and in 1899 he became a young conductor. During his career with the railroad, he married, and the pair had three children. In 1912, Ellis ran for sheriff in a hard-fought election — and won. In 1916, Ellis was defeated in his re-election run for sheriff by J. C. Van Pelt. From 1916–1918, city commissioner Frank Sanders performed the duties of chief of police. On June 10, 1918, Ellis was again appointed chief and held that position until he was again elected sheriff in 1920.

- **Milton Frank, Chief of Police: January 1, 1921–June 10, 1923**

  On December 31, 1920, the former chief of police, Milton Frank, found himself as the department's desk sergeant. His skills that brought him to the position of chief in 1906 got him promoted on that day to Captain. Also, because Chief Cary Ellis had recently been elected sheriff, he stepped down from his chief's position on December 31, 1920. Mr. Frank became acting chief, and later chief.

- **Mose Penton, Chief of Police: June 11, 1923–October 23, 1923**

  Big, tall, and strong — imposing. That is the impression that the Editor of the *Pensacola News Journal* reported on June 13, 1923 regarding new chief of police Mose Penton. "He's businesslike, yet amiable. In fact, his amiability" the reporter silently prophesied, "will be an effective hypodermic to keep up the morale of the police department." During WWI, he served as a private police officer with the Pensacola Shipbuilding Company. Chief Penton, whose agenda made it appear that he was settling in for quite a while, only served four months. On September 26, 1923, Escambia County Sheriff Cary Ellis was killed

Chief Mose Penton

while making an arrest. On October 23, 1923, Penton stepped down from his new chief of police position after Governor Cary Hardee appointed him the new sheriff.

- **Ernest Ellis Harper, Chief of Police: October 23, 1923– November 19, 1925**

On October 15, 1923, *The Pensacola News Journal* reported that Captain Ernest Ellis Harper was appointed the new chief to replace Mose Penton. Chief Harper was born in 1890 in Roberts, Florida. He moved to Pensacola in 1909 and joined the police force two years later. Chief Harper spent time as a patrolman, a turnkey and a motorcycle officer before being promoted to captain and deputy marshal in 1919. When Chief Harper took over, Prohibition was in full force. The nationwide battle was several years old, and Pensacola was no different. Reports named Sanders Beach as being a "point of sale" for illegal alcohol. "The Barn," located at 105 West Jackson Street, was the party headquarters for naval officers and others. The Black Market was very active, delivering shiploads of alcohol to the locals at the sight of the ruins of the battleship U.S.S. Massachusetts in the Gulf of Mexico.

Chief E. E. Harper

On September 25, 1921, Captain Harper's family was enjoying the fall weather at Chumuckla Springs when their 4-year-old daughter became ill. Their daughter, Marguerite, died that evening and was buried in St. John's Cemetery the next day. The service was held in the family home at 702 North "E" Street.

On November 17, 1925, City Commissioner Frank Dent Sanders died after suffering cerebral hemorrhages. Chief Harper was appointed to the commission in his place. He was then reelected in 1929. He went on to become the police commissioner in 1930. In 1932, Harper made an unsuccessful play for Escambia County Sheriff. After his defeat, Harper became a deputy sheriff. Then, on June 6, 1933, tragedy again struck the Harper family. Harpers wife, Amelia Fleming Harper, died at the age of 43.

Harper continued raising his four children as a single father. In addition to Earnest, Amelia and Marguerite, the family consisted of two boys — Edward & Raymond, and two daughters — Dorothy & Jeanette. Note: Harper's son, Raymond C. Harper, decided to follow in his father's footsteps and become a Pensacola police officer.

- **William O'Connell, Chief of Police: November 19, 1925–January 1, 1932**

Chief William O'Connell

Willie O'Connell took over as chief at the age of 42 and remained at the helm initially for 7 years. For 13 months, he served as chief over the detective bureau from January 1, 1932–February 11, 1933. Under his leadership, the department went through the latter years of Prohibition, the crash of the stock market. Automobiles became the primary mode of transportation, thus requiring more traffic lights, traffic officers and traffic charges.

- **Albert Anderson, Chief of Police: January 1, 1932– February 11, 1933**

In 1931, a new "Council-Manager" form of government was ushered in with a new city charter. The new charter provided that a city manager would be hired by the mayor. The city manager would in effect be the CEO of the city, and would have charge over all city departments, including the police department. In response to the new structure, Mayor H. Clay Armstrong sought out and hired George Roark from Beaumont Texas as the new city manager.

Upon his arrival, Mr. Roark turned the police department on its head. Roark transferred Albert Anderson from the head of the water department to the position of chief of police. Anderson had been a Pensacola Police Officer for 12 years, so he was no stranger to being a lawman. As soon as he took over the position, he made drastic changes. In addition to numerous demotions, promotions and transfers, he created a separate entity called the "Detective Bureau" and demoted chief Willie O'Connell to Chief of Detectives over it and subject to the new chief of police. Of course, the many changes brought about by the new city manager and the new chief did not sit well with members of the police department or with citizens of Pensacola. Lawsuits were filed and petitions signed.

Thirteen months later, unrest which had been brewing between City Manager Roark and Chief Anderson came to a head when Roark asked Anderson for his resignation. Anderson refused. The fight was aired in the media, shocking the citizens! Finally, Anderson agreed to a transfer back to the water department. Roark promoted O'Connell back to his position as chief. All previous changes in the department were reversed and everyone took their rightful place. The world was right again.

- **William O'Connell, Chief of Police: January 1, 1932–July 20, 1947**

In total, Chief O'Connell served as Pensacola Police Chief for 21 years, longer than any other chief to date. O'Connell led the department through the last part of the Great Depression, and World War II.

On July 20 at 9:30 PM, Chief O'Connell, after serving as Pensacola Police Chief for 21 years, died at the age of 61 after a brief illness. According to the July 22 edition of the *Pensacola Journal*, Municipal Judge A. Morley Darby cancelled court the day before in honor of the chief. Judge Darby said that the chief was "a grand old fellow who had a humanitarian attitude" and "who always wanted to help not hurt" persons he dealt with. Chief O'Connell's wife had died several years earlier. He was survived by 10 children and several grandchildren. He lived at 129 West Government Street. His funeral took place at his home at 8:45 AM and St. Michael's Catholic Church at 9:00 AM on Friday, July 25, 1947. He is buried at St. Michael's cemetery. He was replaced by Assistant Chief Crosby Hall.

- **Crosby Hall, Chief of Police: July 21, 1947–October 15, 1961**
On June 14, 1947, Crosby Hall was officially named Assistant Chief of Police. He had been acting as the chief in the absence of Chief O'Connell since he was admitted into a hospital in New Orleans, where he died on July 20. On July 25, Hall was appointed chief of police by city manager Oliver J. Semmes. Hall, a military veteran, had been with the police force for 22 years. He was married and had two children.

Chief Crosby Hall

By 1961, corruption within the Pensacola Police Department had become rampant. The citizens and city fathers of Pensacola were confused and frustrated, as criticism abounded from all walks of the community. City Manager Homer D. Reed finally asked Crosby Hall for his resignation as chief. On October 15, 1961, Chief Hall resigned, mostly due to the cloud that hung over the department. Clyde Lewis served as interim police chief. Chief Hall and his wife continued to live in Pensacola at 2012 N Baylen Street and participate in community events. His wife, Lucy Penton Hall, died October 8, 1970. After her death, Chief Hall moved into a room at the St. Carlos Hotel. He was found dead on December 29, 1971, reportedly from natural causes. He was 67 years old.

- **Drexel P. Caldwell, Chief of Police: February 2, 1962–July 12, 1974**
Drexel P. Caldwell was born in Luverne, Alabama in 1914. He joined the Pensacola Police Department in 1946 after his discharge from the U. S. Army. He was promoted to sergeant on April 24, 1952. On February 3, 1962, Caldwell was named Chief of Police over a department riddled with corruption, after Chief Crosby Hall was asked to resign.

After the retirement of Chief Hall, the Pensacola City Council discussed the procedure for choosing the next chief. An outside firm was hired to handle the procedure. The firm selected three finalists: Inspector Clyde Lewis, Captain James Davis, and Sergeant Drexel Caldwell. After many months and tests, the firm decided. At four o'clock in the afternoon on Friday, February 2, 1962, Pensacola City Manager Homer Reed named Sergeant Drexel P. Caldwell Chief of Police. Reed said that Caldwell was best suited to accomplish three immediate needs — department reorganization, increased training, and rebuilding public confidence in the department. In addition to building the public's confidence, Chief Caldwell had to rebuild the officers' confidence in their leadership. Morale was low. He began by demanding more professionalism in their demeanor, dress, appearance, and communication. He also instituted a retirement fund for the officers. Of the three needs, the most time-consuming was rebuilding the officers' lost confidence. But he was ready for the task.

Chief Drexel P. Caldwell

Chief Caldwell set in to make the department more professional. He was one of the leading police chiefs in Florida to demand more professionalism and training for his officers. Less than three weeks after his appointment, his officers were in training classes learning about the latest traffic laws.

On March 27, 1962, Chief Caldwell gave a presentation to the Pensacola City Council's Committee of the Whole regarding the reorganization of the entire department. If approved, the department would operate under three divisions instead of the current four. Several positions and ranks were reassigned, a medical examiner hired, the position of assistant chief abolished, an administrative assistant appointed to the chief, and a dispatch unit was recommended. All the changes and purchase of new cruisers came at a price tag of $35,000. Reorganizing the department gave officers comfort to put their trust in their supervisors. The committee voted 6–1 for approval. Officers underwent riot control training and classes in dealing with the public. This training increased the citizens' confidence level in their department.

In 1974, Caldwell was ready to retire. In the words of city manager Frank Faison, "Chief Caldwell has moved the police division from the low public opinion in the early 1960s to a first-rate organization." Caldwell's last day was July 12, 1974.

- **James Davis, Chief of Police: July 12, 1974–August 22, 1980**
On June 4, 1974, Pensacola City Manager Frank Faison called a press conference in which he, Chief Caldwell, and Assistant Chief James Davis were present. Faison announced the resignation of Drexel Caldwell as chief. Caldwell stated that he had made the decision to resign to run for the state senate. Faison also announced that he intended to appoint Davis as Caldwell's successor.

On Friday, July 12, 1974, the ceremony that took place in front 40 South Alcaniz Street was not a typical retirement ceremony. Neither was it a typical installation for a new chief of police. It was a "changing of the guard" ceremony. It involved both outgoing Chief Caldwell's retirement and incoming Chief Davis' installment. Caldwell thanked his officers and spoke

City Manager Frank Faison, new Chief James Davis, and Outgoing Chief D.P. Caldwell

his confidence in his successor, an old friend and former walking beat partner. Davis thanked his predecessor for leaving him a department in good shape.

Chief Davis already had a reputation among the officers for being intelligent and professional. He joined the department in 1946 — 28 years before making chief. Mild-mannered, Davis received a master's degree from the University of West Florida and graduated with honors. He had been to the FBI National Academy and was a member of the FBI National Academy Associates. He was on the Board of Directors of East Hill Baptist Church and had an impeccable record at the Pensacola Police Department. Davis had earned the top score of the chief's exam in 1962, when Caldwell became chief.

Davis had to hit the ground running. As he took over, the racial riots were in full swing. Also, the United States' involvement in the Vietnam War was ending, so veterans were returning home. Consequently, illegal drug use was gaining popularity. Marijuana, which had been enjoying widespread use for about 10 years, was joined by hashish, heroin, LSD, and cocaine. All these drugs had been used and misused for many years, but the consumption of illegal drugs emerged as a major problem for the Pensacola Police during this time. The new chief met these challenges head-on.

- **Louis Goss, Chief of Police: August 22, 1980–December 31, 1994**
  The Thursday, June 19, 1980 edition of the *Pensacola News Journal* reported "Chief Interviews." The article announced the retirement of Chief James Davis and that his successor would be chosen from these applicants: Jim Billy Barnes, Glen Darling, Louis Goss, John Haner, George Underwood, Herb Seely, Richard Fuller, and Richard Yelverton. August 22 was to be Davis's last day. He was 62 years old, with 34 ½ years on the force. He had held the top position since 1974. His plans were to simply…be retired. After thorough testing, interviews, and research

into the background of each candidate, a decision was made. Manager Faison announced the Louis Goss would be the new chief. Chief Davis would transfer command to Captain Goss at a ceremony at the Sheraton Inn, Alcaniz and Garden Streets on August 22, 1980.

February 1925 — Forest, Mississippi: Louis Goss was born in a small, rural logging town. He grew up working in the logging camps. His family moved to Walnut Hill where he grew to manhood. In 1943, he was drafted and fought in WWII. After the war, he met and married his wife Ruth. He joined the Pensacola Police Department on June 6, 1946 at the age of 21. In 1958, he was promoted to sergeant, lieutenant in 1965, and captain in 1971. In an interview with the media, Goss said he felt his autocratic style of leadership fit police work.

l-r: Chiefs Lou Goss, D. P. Caldwell, James Davis

Shortly after his swearing-in ceremony and celebration, Chief Goss performed his first action. He left the celebration, crossed the street to the police station, called in Officer David Lee, and fired him. Officer Lee was a member of the Florida National Guard and had stayed with his unit longer than the time agreed upon. Goss received a lot of criticism from department members and the public for firing Lee.

As chief, Lou Goss implemented the department's K-9 Unit, and started the Field Training Program. Upon graduating from the police academy, every officer underwent supervised, hands-on instruction to help the officer get a feel of the job. The field Training program substantially improved the training and lowered the liability to the department.

- **Norman Chapman, Chief of Police: December 31, 1994– October 14, 1998**

Lou Goss remained in the chief of police position for his last 14 years of a 48-year career as a Pensacola Police Officer. Under Chief Goss' leadership, the department moved into the new headquarters and the department expanded. New programs were begun, including the DARE program in the schools, specially trained officers in the housing developments, and the PPD Dive Team. After nearly 50 years of serving the citizens of Pensacola, On December 31, 1994, all available members of the police department fell into formation in the front of the new police station for the change of command. Chief Goss, who was in uniform, spoke of his time with the department. Then, Judge Lacey Collier administered the oath of office to incoming Chief Norman Chapman. Chapman, 51 years old, was an 18-year member of the Department. The final act of the day was when city officials named the new police station "The Louis Goss Police Headquarters." A few weeks later, Sgt Jerry Potts was promoted to the position of Assistant Chief.

Chief Norman Chapman

Chief Chapman initiated a program that assigned police vehicles to every officer. He expanded the new K-9 corps and reorganized several sections within the department. The changes increased morale throughout the department. Ironically, Norman Chapman was the detective who investigated the case of Ted Bundy. During their interview, Bundy told Chapman "Norman, this is going to make you chief." On October 14, 1998, after only four years, Norman Chapman retired the chief's position for health reasons. Assistant Chief Jerry Potts served as acting chief until a successor was named.

- **Jerry Potts, Chief of Police: October 14, 1998–March 29, 2002**

On March 27, 1948, Jerry Potts was born in Pensacola, where he grew up in and attended school. In middle school, he met his future wife, Linda. While in high school, Jerry recognized that tensions were escalating overseas in Vietnam. The United States was becoming more involved daily. After high school in 1965, Jerry joined the U. S. Army. He married Linda the following year — on August 26, 1966. Jerry went on to become an airborne soldier with the famous 82nd Airborne Division. He earned the Combat Infantry Badge before receiving an honorable discharge in 1968. On May 21, 1973, Jerry was sworn in as a police officer under Chief James Davis.

Jerry was not only a likeable officer, but he was intelligent, often using his gift for communicating to solve problems. He was one of those guys that could put someone in jail and the suspect would thank him for it!

Jerry was soon promoted to sergeant. Shortly afterwards, he found his niche. He was assigned to supervise the traffic section. The traffic section essentially served as the traffic, escort, public relations, and event coordination section. Jerry was not only called on to attend countless meetings, but he also spoke at many banquets and events, made television appearances, and served as the Department's Public Information Officer. As such, he served as Assistant Chief of Police.

On Sunday, January 31, 1999, City Manager Tom Bonfield called Jerry Potts at home. Bonfield had been working through the process of making the best choice for chief since Norman Chapman retired October 14, 1998. Jerry had been serving as the acting chief since Chapman stepped down. Bonfield began with eight applicants, narrowed the list to three, and chose Jerry Potts, 50, a 26-year

Chief Jerry Potts

veteran law officer. When he called Potts and offered him the position, Potts accepted. Chief Potts was a familiar face and well-liked throughout town. In addition to being the department spokesperson, Potts was the host of the department's weekly television show. Numerous letters of support for Potts were sent to Mr. Bonfield from citizens. He was forever remembered by the ivory-handled chrome revolver he wore, even though most officers had transitioned to semi-automatics. People often came up to him and said "Wow, I really like your pearl-handled revolver," to which Jerri always courteously replied "It's not pearl — it's ivory." Chief Potts' induction ceremony took place at 10 AM at the police station.

After four years as chief, Jerry Potts announced his retirement. As if he knew there would be questions, he added that he just wanted to spend time with his wife, both at home and traveling. On March 29, 2002, Chief Potts left his office for the last time. He died of cancer on August 6, 2010.

- **John Mathis, Chief of Police: April 8, 2002–June 11, 2010**
  Almost immediately after Jerry Potts submitted his resignation, City Manager Tom Bonfield began the search for a replacement. It was Mr. Bonfield's desire to, for the first time, look inside and outside the department for a replacement. Before long, 70 applications arrived on his desk. Mr. Bonfield appointed committees to look over the applicants and to question who they thought would be the best fit. The list was narrowed to three. Finally, on March 27, the announcement was made for the new chief position — John Mathis. John, 45 years old, became the department's chief at a ceremony on April 8, 2002, at the Pensacola Police Department. U.S. District Judge Lacey Collier administered the oath of office, and Mayor John Fogg was

Chief John Mathis

the guest speaker at the 2 PM ceremony. Chief Mathis brought with him support not only from the public but also from within the ranks. Chief Mathis had been a Pensacola Police Officer for 27 years. He was married to Sue Saffran and they had four children. Chief Mathis listed community policing efforts as his priority. Under his command, the Neighborhood Policing Unit enlarged and became a division within the department. He secured funding for officers to have video cameras in patrol cars. Chief Mathis promoted Captain Chip Simmons to Assistant Chief. On June 11, 2010, Chief Mathis retired. "I've had a rewarding career. It's just time to draw it to an end. This is about what I had planned all along."

- **Chip Simmons, Chief of Police: March 28, 2011–July 15, 2015**
When Chief Mathis cleaned out his office, he left Assistant Chief Chip Simmons in charge as Interim chief. Chief Simmons joined the department in 1986. He was 46 years old when he was appointed interim chief. As a result of the new form of city government voted in by the citizens, Mayor Ashton Hayward took the helms of the mayor's office. His first order of business was to appoint a chief of police. On March 28, 2011, Simmons was named the next chief. On April 12, a reception in his honor took place at the Sanders Beach Corrine Jones Center.

Chief Chip Simmons

Under Chief Simmons' leadership, the department achieved accreditation status for the first time. Accreditation brings a department in line with department expectations and standards across the nation. In addition, Pensacola Police Officers began wearing bodycams on their uniforms. Chief Simmons retired on July 15, 2015.

- **David Alexander, Chief of Police: July 16, 2015–May 12, 2017**
Born in Our Lady of Angels Clinic in Pensacola, David Alexander III is the oldest of five children. His hard-working parents, David Alexander

Jr., a factory worker, and Annie M., a janitor, devoted themselves to teaching all five children good Christian values and instilled in them the meaning of hard work. David remembered these lessons and took them very seriously. David was the first in his family to earn a college degree. David's career in public life began in Pensacola as a public safety cadet, working for the City of Pensacola Police Department. In David's cadet interview he was asked "Where do you see yourself in five years?" His answer was "sergeant, lieutenant, or even captain." David was very ambitious and aspired to move up the career ladder. Despite seeing few black men in the ranks of law enforcement, David was proud to join the Pensacola Police Department. He earned the reputation of being an officer with integrity and was known by all for his fairness.

Chief David Alexander

It was that type of character that helped him move through the ranks. During his 32 years of service, he served in every capacity of the police department. In 2017, David Alexander III made history in Pensacola, Florida when he was appointed the City of Pensacola's first African American police chief.

As chief of police, David was praised for his servant-leadership and a significant reduction in crime. David led the department through the staffing crisis and despite the budget constraints, he kept officers on the streets to respond to calls for services. Remarkably, through increased positive interactions with citizens and community policing, crime was reduced an additional 10.2 percent, bringing the crime rate to the lowest it had been in 20 years.

Chief Alexander's "Intentional Policing Strategies" were known for innovative programs like *Kids and Cops* and *BLAST*, mentoring programs that empowered at risk students through tutoring, community service, and other positive incentives. The *Kids and Cops* program introduced youth to civic engagement along with the importance of a quality education. It also rewarded them with a trip to the state capitol, a state university college visit, and an all-day experience at Tampa's Bush Gardens. The *BLAST* program was a partnership with the Department of Justice to build lasting relationships between police and citizens. This program was initially launched at Camelot Academy, a school stigmatized for having students who had learning challenges to overcome. The program was not only successful, but it was part of the recognition given to the Pensacola Police Department in the 2016 International Association of Police Chiefs Conference in San Diego, California. This program served as a model strategy for 21st Century Community Policing. Chief Alexander launched a "Literacy Free Library" project to reintroduce literacy in some of the area's most crime ridden neighborhoods. Chief Alexander collaborated with faith leaders, city officials, elected officials, and citizens to improve the quality of life in neighborhoods distressed by violent crimes.

Chief Alexander implemented other innovative ideas, such as: Coffee with a Cop, Gifts and Toys at Christmas, Stop and Talk, Community United in Prayer events, town hall meetings, radio talk shows, Race and Reconciliation, Youth & Police Academy, Big Brothers Big Sisters' Bigs and Badges, Florida Youth Challenge Academy, LETF grants to the public, and TV public safety campaign ads. He successfully united law enforcement and citizens to achieve what agencies and departments across the nation were struggling to acquire: a good police-community relation and a haven for all its citizens.

Alexander has received numerous awards and recognitions for his outstanding commitment to serving the community. He was honored by the Most Worshipful Grand Master Walter Gulley, of the Most Worshipful Union Grand Lodge of Florida-Belize, Central America Jurisdiction, for his overall professional law enforcement achievements. He also received the Presidential Lifetime Achievement Award.

Chief Alexander retired in May of 2017, but remained involved in the community, collaborating with others to create positive change and make a difference in the people's lives.

- **Tommi Lyter, Chief of Police: May 12, 2017 –**
On Friday, May 12, 2017, Chief David Alexander stepped down, and Assistant Chief Tommi Lyter assumed the position of chief. The son of a Navy father, Lyter was born in Lewiston, Pennsylvania on March 16th, 1969. As a child, he lived in Virginia Beach, Maine, New Jersey, Atsugi, Japan, and Pensacola, where he graduated high school. For most of his life, Chief Lyter desired to be a police officer. While still in high school, he made the commitment to pursue a career in law enforcement, enrolling in the Criminal Justice program at Pensacola State College after high school.

Chief Tommi Lyter

Chief Lyter joined the Pensacola Police Department on August 13, 1990. His favorite assignments included working as a K-9 officer and SWAT team member, but the best job he ever held was that of a patrol sergeant. Tommi worked his way through the ranks, attaining the rank of assistant chief in 2015. Chief Lyter and his wife, Brenda are the parents of Christopher, Jonathan, and Brandon.

"I've worked with some of the greatest people to ever wear a police uniform and I've made some of the best friends I could ever ask for" was Tommi's answer when asked what the best thing was about working at the Pensacola Police Department. The low points were witnessing severe injuries and death to children.

When asked about the changes in the police profession he had seen over his career, the chief answered "Computer technology has changed drastically over the years. It's helped make our jobs easier and more efficient. I believe that our job is much harder today because of the added demands placed on officers and public scrutiny."

On Friday, May 26, Tommi's wife, Brenda, held the Bible while Tommi took the oath of office administered by Escambia County Judge Amy Brodersen at Olive Baptist Church.

On October 12, 2019, tragedy struck. Chief Lyter's wife, Brenda, lost her battle to cancer at the young age of 51. She passed away peacefully with her family surrounding her. As expected, the family mourned and Chief Lyter's family of officers mourned with them.

STORIES

Suicide or Murder?

He is known as Pensacola's leading citizen. Through the tumultuous years of British rule in Pensacola, Elias Durnford was the glue that held the town together. Elias Durnford was born on June 13, 1739 in Ringwood, UK. As the intelligent young man, he was, he decided to pursue a commission in the British Army as a civil engineer. After spending several years in the military — mostly aboard ships — Durnford's talents were realized when he was assigned to the new frontier town of Pensacola. He accepted the assignment with enthusiasm and, upon his arrival in 1764, he immediately began laying out a grid for a proper British town. It was then that he met his two leaders, Governor George Johnstone, and Lt. Governor Monforte Browne.

George Johnstone was born in Dumfriesshire in 1730. A proven brilliant leader in battle, Johnstone was outspoken and often found himself at odds with his superiors. Although he commanded men and ships during battle, he was not well-liked. He was involved in several duels and was even accused of bribery. When he was promoted to Governor of West Florida in 1764, his naval career had already spanned 19 years. While governor in West Florida, he openly kept a concubine by the name of Martha Ford, with whom he sired four children. Because of his combative personality, it was a surprise to no one that he and his lieutenant, Montfort Browne, did not get along.

Montfort Browne was Irish, from Cornwall. He served with the 35th Regiment of Foot during the seven year's war (1756–1763). His career suffered when a court of inquiry ruled against him in 1763. He found solace through an appointment as lieutenant governor of British West Florida. Upon his arrival in the capitol village of Pensacola, he began to have difficulties with Governor Johnstone, his immediate superior. Besides his increasingly strained relationship with his boss, he was investigated by British officials for unscrupulous bookkeeping irregularities.

As far as anyone knows, Johnstone and Browne never got along with each other — ever. Browne even filed complaints on Johnstone to the British Crown. Finally, in 1767, the British Crown recalled Johnstone home to answer those complaints. This, of course, left Monfort Browne as acting governor of west Florida. Further, it caused Browne to consider that he might be appointed governor permanently, which may have been his motivation all along for filing the complaints.

John Eliot was born on June 2, 1742 in Port Eliot, St Germans, Cornwall of an influential family. At the young age of 10, he was already a midshipman, and a 3rd Lieutenant at age 15. In this position, he worked on the Augusta for George Johnstone. Soon, Her Majesty's Navy retained Eliot as Captain. He commanded several ships from 1759–1766. During this time, he and his crew were taken captive by French privateers. His family paid for his freedom, but he was praised by his crew and superiors for his heroic actions during captivity. On March 16, 1767, John Eliot was recommended for the new governor position of the frontier settlement of west Florida. After the Earl of Shelburne considered his choices, he appointed Eliot, effective immediately.

British West Florida

In the two years since Browne had removed rival Johnstone, he no doubt thought about ways to obtain the title of governor. On Sunday, April 2, 1769, while Browne was nearby in Mobile, Alabama, Governor Eliot arrived. With the help of Elias Durnford, Eliot settled in and began to set up his office. A few days later, Browne returned home to find that he was no longer acting governor. His dreams of occupying the office of governor were suddenly crushed. Moreover, Browne learned that Eliot had launched an investigation into his behavior toward Johnstone. "Because of this young man — this junior officer, I will not be governor and will probably be stripped of my position as lieutenant governor." Browne must have said to himself. "What can be done?" But…maybe something.

On Monday, May 1, 1769, Eliot brought Monforte Browne into his office for an interrogation. No record exists of the interview, but it was most assuredly not agreeable — no doubt heated. Eliot made accusations toward Browne about his conduct. Meanwhile, the entire community held its collective breath. The encounter between the top ranked officials in their town was taking place, and it was not pleasant. The record shows that the two men had dinner at Eliot's quarters, and Eliot interrogated Browne well into the night. John Eliot was never seen alive again.

Eliot could not be located the next morning, so a search was organized. The 27-year-old governor was found in his office, dead. He had been lynched. Browne, now self-appointed acting governor, proclaimed Eliot's death a suicide. Browne said that he had been with Eliot "dining and spending time with him" and was surprised that he would end his life.[12] Despite any evidence or the townspeople's suspicions, Browne was never charged. With Eliot's dispatch, the investigation regarding Browne's conduct went away.

Monfort Browne was renamed temporary governor. However, colonists in Pensacola filed numerous complaints regarding Browne to England. Browne sent his newly appointed lieutenant governor, Elias Durnford, to England to answer the charges.

While he was in England, Durnford met a young lady named Rebecca Walker. After a short romance, the two were married on August 25, 1769. Rebecca accompanied Elias to their new home in West Florida. Besides a new wife, Durnford returned with more news — his own appointment as governor.

Monforte Browne was finally ousted from his position and from Pensacola. While preparing to leave, Browne became involved in a dispute with a local trader and challenged him to a duel. The duel took place and Browne prevailed but did not kill his opponent. He was detained in Pensacola until his victim's survival was obvious. On August 29, 1778, Browne participated in the famous siege of Rhode Island. Afterwards, accusations of cowardice and incompetence were brought against him. Consequently, he was removed from office permanently. He died two years later.

Governor George Johnstone retired, and lived a quiet life. He died of throat cancer on May 24, 1787.

Elias Durnford and his wife, Rebecca decided to make Pensacola their permanent home.

When Governor Peter Chester arrived, he calmed matters. Durnford was still a trusted confidant, serving as governor until the arrival of Chester on August 10, 1770. Afterwards, he and Rebecca enjoyed their nine children. Durnford served on the West Florida Council until 1778. He died on June 11, 1794 in Trinidad.

First Prisoner of Distinction

Pensacola's first city jail was no more than a previous soldiers' quarters with a guard stationed outside. However, a month after Pensacola became an American town, the jail housed its first celebrity, in August of 1821. As soon as the new government was established, disputes over land grants surfaced. Some of the new Americans laid claim to the tracts previously owned by wealthy Spaniards. In one of the disputes, a woman came before Judge Brackenridge with a complaint that the land willed to her had been taken by the local traders Panton, Leslie, and Co. She took the case to the Spanish court who ruled in her favor but would not enforce the ruling. The answers to this claim and many of the others lay in the papers that were in the possession of Domingo Sousa, lieutenant of the former Spanish governor, Colonel Jose Callava. Both men were still in town. When Judge Brackenridge and his American officials demanded the papers, the lieutenant claimed he did not have the authority to release them. He then took the papers to the home of Callava for safekeeping. Governor Andrew Jackson, who was not fond of Callava, inserted himself into the matter. He sent a contingent to Callava's home, demanding that he release the papers. Callava tauntingly refused, claiming both illness and diplomatic immunity. He also said he could not understand the English demand, nor the translators that came with them. Finally, he claimed that he knew nothing about the papers in question. Brackenridge and his men searched through the papers and found the ones associated with the complainant, but Callava would not release them. This made Governor Jackson furious. He summoned Callava to his office. A "colorful" dispute took place between the current and former governor (accounts differed) and ended with Jackson ordering the arrest of the Spaniard and some of his men[18]. Jackson also dispatched officials to Callava's home to confiscate the papers. A jovial Colonel Callava and his men were taken to the abandoned soldiers' barracks and jailed there. The quarters were old, dirty, not sufficient, and beneath the colonel, according to one of his men. The guards reported overhearing the prisoners laughing at Jackson's manner and mocking him. As they occupied the large cell, chairs, tables, candles food and wine were brought in by the Spaniards who had remained in Pensacola. In other words, the prisoners enjoyed the sentence they received. They were released the following day.

Old Jail Cell Window

After a long stay from April to October in Pensacola, the Jacksons were eager to get home. Rachel left Pensacola on October 1, 1821, for her home in Nashville. General Jackson followed a few weeks later. His resignation letter as governor of the territories of East and West Florida soon followed.

Pensacola's Escape Artist

The Old Spanish Trail had been around since before the Spanish first appeared in West Florida in 1559. It had been used for many years by the Native Americans. It was the only road from Pensacola to St. Augustine. Everyone who made the trip took that route — traders, settlers, politicians, and messengers. Colonel Andrew Jackson even took it. It was later lengthened west to New Orleans, and then much later, when automobiles came on the scene, to California.

Thomas Jones was an official mail carrier for West Florida. He regularly made the trip from Alaqua (Walton County) to Pensacola and back again with bags full of mail. The well-worn trail was fraught with many dangers and obstacles, including deadly encounters from Native Americans, rivers and streams that had to be crossed, and wild animal attacks. The two-day trip was precarious, even for a veteran traveler such as Jones.

On July 14, 1827, while Jones was on the trail, two men approached him, one of whom had a gun, and the other holding a knife. The man with the gun shot at Jones, missing his head by less than an inch. The other man stabbed at him, but only ripped his clothes. Jones managed to escape to the nearest town and report the incident.

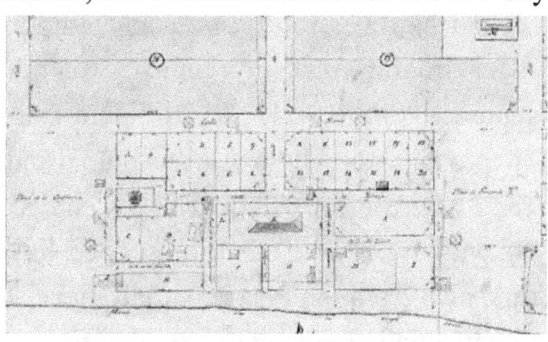
1813 Map of Pensacola by Vincente Pintado. The jail is labeled "M" at Alcaniz and Intendencia

A manhunt ensued. Identifying one of the attackers was an easy task for the officials, especially since Martin Hutto had committed such crimes many times in the past. He was apprehended, arrested, and transported to the only jail in West Florida — the one in Pensacola.

The old jail wasn't much. In fact, it was badly in need of repair. Vincent Pintado, a local mapmaker, had created a Pensacola map in 1813 which showed a "Public Prison." This jail, located at Alcaniz and Intendencia Streets, was recorded by a local newspaper in 1827 as being in deplorable condition. Therefore, it was no surprise when it was discovered that Hutto had escaped. On September 5, 1827, a reward of $80 was offered for his apprehension. He was suspected of fleeing to Butler County, Alabama.

In November, Hutto voluntarily turned himself in, anticipating an acquittal when the judge came into town later that month and held court. Unfortunately, Judge Brackenridge did not come for his usual November hearings, so Hutto had to wait until May of 1828. Fearing that Hutto would escape again, he was held in the military jail at the US Army camp known as Cantonment Clinch, located on the shore of Bayou Chico.

Hutto escaped from the Army jail on January 23, 1828. A reward of $30 was offered this time. Hutto was quickly recaptured and stood trial on May 7, 1828. A jury found him guilty and he was held in the jail while awaiting his sentence. On May 15, Hutto again escaped. A fifty-dollar reward was offered this time. Hutto was recaptured and returned to Pensacola in October 1828 where Judge Brackenridge sentenced Hutto to two years in prison. On March 27, 1829, Hutto escaped for the fourth and last time — this time also from the Pensacola jail, never to be heard from again. The city fathers finally realized that they needed to address the problem of the old, inadequate, jail.

The Branded Hand

In 1844, the issue of slavery was taking place in Pensacola. Like most southern towns, some slaves lived in Pensacola, but not as many as a lot of places in the South. Because Pensacola was different from most southern towns — mostly due to the presence of the military — pro-slavery sentiments abounded. A few of the wealthy landowners owned many slaves, upward near 60. The vast majority of the city's residents did not own any slaves. Many were vehemently opposed to the idea of one human being owning another.

The Trial of Jonathan Walker

Jonathan Walker was a white man who lived in Pensacola and opposed slavery. Walker, originally from Massachusetts, was a devout Christian who did not believe that one person should own another one, even though it happened in Bible times.

On June 22, 1844, Walker boarded a boat occupied by several black men. The destination was Nassau, The Bahamas, where the men would find freedom — thanks to Walker. Even though slaves regularly came and went throughout Pensacola, the discovery of the slaves' disappearance caused fingers to be pointed at law enforcement. The June 29th edition of the *Pensacola Gazette* issued a scathing editorial criticizing the Pensacola police for not catching the slaves before they boarded the boat.

Of course, sailing in the warm waters of the Gulf in July caused many of the men to become ill, making for a long and turbulent journey. Further, on July 8, the captain and crew of the schooner *Eliza Catharine* stopped and boarded Walker's boat. Believing that Walker was helping enslaved people to freedom, the captain escorted the boat to Key West, where he appeared before a magistrate. Walker was ordered to be returned to Pensacola to stand trial. He arrived in Pensacola on July 19, met by Deputy U. S. Marshal James Gonzales, who Walker said treated him humanely.

Walker was convinced that the courts would have no choice but to see that a person's freedom is more important than another person's property. He was wrong. After half an hour, the jury came back with a verdict of guilty. The sentence was unusual in today's terms. Walker received from the judge fifteen days imprisonment, be locked in the pillory, and exposed to thrown rotten eggs and garbage for an hour and have "SS" for *Slave Stealer* branded into the palm of his right hand. He was also ordered to pay a $150 fine.

The accepted practice for the hour in the pillory was to cover the head of the accused. As Walker's head was being covered, the owner of two of the men who escaped — George Willis — pulled off the cover and threw rotten eggs at him. After his hour, he washed up and was taken to the courtroom. His hand was tied to a post and U. S. Marshal Ebenezer Dorr sizzled the brand onto his palm for 20 seconds, while a silent Walker remained still.

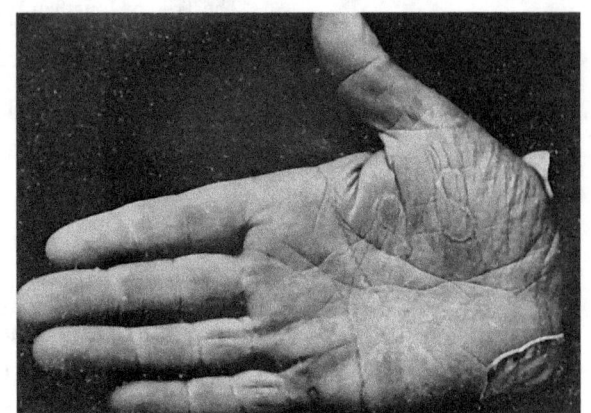

Jonathan Walker's left hand with the "SS" branded on it

The judge then sentenced Walker to incarceration for 15 days. The trial made national news. The case of Jonathan Walker occurred during a time when it was assumed that most northerners were against slavery, while it appeared that most southerners were pro-slavery, once again, Pensacola was not typical. Protests against the arrest and sentence of Walker ensued throughout the town and, eventually, the country. The basis of the protests was that slaves are people and should not be bought and sold as property and that Walker's efforts to assist another person to freedom was more important than a person losing property.

A book entitled *The Branded Hand; The Trial and Imprisonment of Jonathan Walker* was written by the prisoner and enjoyed immense popularity nationwide, as did a poem entitled *The Man with the Branded Hand* — written by John Greenleaf. These brought national attention to

Walker, to the case, and to Pensacola. It quite possibly also brought national attention to the issue of slavery, helping to usher in the Civil War.

Jonathan Walker

Jonathan Walker, a man of great discipline, had a habit that benefits us today. He kept a daily journal of his experiences, including his stay at the Pensacola prison. He describe the jail as follows: "The jail is a brick building of two stories, about eighteen by thirty-six feet, having upon each floor two rooms, the lower part for the occupation of the prisoners, and the upper part for the jailer's family. The rooms for the prisoners are fifteen to sixteen feet square, with double doors, and two small grated windows from six to eight feet from the lower floor. Overhead is a single board floor, which but little obstructs the noise of the upper part from being distinctly heard below, and vice versa."

On February 5, 1846 (1½ years after his sentence), Walker escaped his cell, using a pickaxe that was given to him by a friend. He was caught and forced to pay a fine. He left Pensacola, never to return.

Dueling Oaks

Historically, men have settled their differences through combat. The tradition of the honorable manner has certainly changed over the years. In today's culture, if one man offends or insults another, fists will fly…or worse. Not long ago, the words "Let's take it outside!" were heard. In medieval Europe, the honored tradition of dueling became popular. This continued into the new world, especially among members of the military. In the Old South, when one gentleman besmirched another — especially regarding his wife — the offended party was expected

Dueling Pistols

to show great indignation, saying something like "Ah dumand satisfaction, Suh!" Interpreted, this meant an apology, explanation, or proof of the offense was expected to be provided. The satisfaction could be immediate, or it could come within a day or two, giving the offender time to gather his evidence, give his apology — written or verbal — or explain his remark. However, if the offending party was unable offer proof, and could not or would not explain or apologize, it was part of "The Code" of a gentleman to challenge the offender to a duel. If the challenge was not accepted, the challenged offender would be considered a coward, and the practice of "posting" — posting a declaration in several public places that the man was a coward — took place. If he accepted the challenge, written accounts of the incident were requested from participants and witnesses who were present at the time of the offense. This was required so that it would be clear that there was an intentional affront, that the insult was meant to be — an insult. If the challenge and acceptance stood, a time and place would be agreed on. This administrative work was carried out by each duelist's *second*. A *second* was a friend or colleague chosen by each man to communicate, clarify and, if possible mediate. If the duel occurred, the *second* stood aside to shoot the opponent if he cheated. The challenged person chose the type of weapon — pistols, long guns, swords, knives, daggers, axes, or clubs could be used. Sometimes, a pair of dueling pistols or swords was provided, and these could be expensive — according to the status of the participants. Most of the time, though, each man used his own weapon. Pistols were used most.

Often, according to the popularity of the duelists, a crowd would gather to watch. Occasionally, the challenge became quite the social event. If possible, a surgeon was on hand to patch up one or both parties. The parties stood an agreed distance apart, and the *seconds* would, one last time, ensure that this was the last resort. If so, the duel would begin. With bladed weapons, the duel proceeded much like what we know as a knife fight, with both parties circling and trying to find an opportunity to cut the other. However, if firearms were used in the duel, both parties had to stand still and take the shot of the other while shooting. The challenged shot first. Hit or miss, the challenger shot next, if he was able. To feint, duck or run-for-cover was considered cowardly. Usually, if conflict went this far, both parties would be shot — maybe killed. Often one was shot and the other killed. The "winner" was often arrested and, if the "loser" died, the winner was charged with murder. Bad outcomes on both ends.

During the 1800s, duels became outlawed in many communities, although the laws did little to curb the practice. Popular opinion ruled. Dueling in Florida became illegal on December 28, 1824 — it was considered murder. If a duel was said to be scheduled, the local police showed up and stopped it, arresting one or both parties if necessary. Often, the police were not aware of the scheduled incident, arrived too late, or chose to turn a blind eye to the matter if they felt it should proceed. However, when the War between the States was over, many people reconsidered the value of human life, and the popularity of duels declined.

In Pensacola, a location was set aside for duels, a beautiful spot on the southeastern corner of town, known as *Dueling Oaks*. The place — covered in gorgeous live oaks — overlooks Pensacola Bay, near the more modern 17th Avenue Trestle. As was stated many times, it is truly a beautiful spot to die. Most of the challenges were not as formal as described above. Often, the challenged talked it out, exchanged money, or fought it out. However, if a duel was scheduled, *everyone* knew where it would be, including the police. There are instances of duels being fought in other locations, however. Palafox Street is one example.

There exists an account of a young lieutenant in General Andrew Jackson's regiment who was challenged to a duel and was killed. Jackson reportedly was very fond of the young man. This was another reason that Jackson was keen to leave Pensacola.

Stephen Mallory, a man from Key West, met a young lady named Angela Moreno, of the wealthy Moreno family of Pensacola. After they wed, the couple raised a family (9 children) in Monroe County, Florida. Stephen held several government offices, including United States senator from Florida. When the Civil War broke out, he was appointed Secretary of the Navy of the Confederacy by President Jefferson Davis. At the end of the war, Mallory spent a year in prison for treason. After his release, he returned to live with his family in Pensacola, unable to hold office. Returning to practice law in Pensacola, he ironically became an outspoken proponent for the education of African Americans, who were now free.

Stephen Mallory

This caused problems between Mallory and the local newspapers. William Kirk, a local editor, was critical of Mallory's actions, and his attacks were often personal. On May 7, 1868, Kirk took offense to some of Mallory's statements and challenged him to a duel at The Dueling Oaks. When the challenge was discovered, officers from the Pensacola Police Department arrested Mr. Kirk. As soon as Kirk was released, he challenged Mallory again at the same location. A constable was summoned and arrived just in time to stop the duel before the shooting began.

On March 4, 1881, the Pensacola and Atlantic Railroad came into existence, and began construction on June 1 of the same year. The track ran through the middle of Dueling Oaks and across the 17th Avenue trestle, also known as Graffiti Bridge. Later, the southern half was made into Frascati Park and the northern half was eventually purchased by the Wilder family.

Okay, admit it. As primitive as it sounds, there is something about a duel that is exciting and manly. Some say that boxing matches, wrestling matches and other sports have taken the place of duels. Uh…NO! What about golf? Video games? COME ON!!!

Police Duties

Privies: In the days before indoor plumbing, citizens either drew water from a well or carried it from one of the creeks located in each end of town. Of course, indoor bathrooms did not exist. Privies (outhouses) were used. On July 17, 1824, the *Pensacola Gazette* published a city ordinance enacted on November 16, 1822, stating that all privies within the city limits of Pensacola be at least 3 feet deep. Those less than that depth by January 1, 1823, would be fined $5. If the owner of the privy continued to ignore the ordinance, the city would dig it out and charge the owner for the work. The police had the job of measuring the privy and ensuring it met the minimum.

Hogs & Goats: Officials passed a city ordinance on April 14, 1834 that required everyone within the city limits to keep his or her hogs & goats tied up. Any hogs or goats found loose would be rounded up…by the police. The police would then hold the wandering hogs & goats at the police station and keep them while an ad was placed in the local paper. The owner was to pay the fine and pick up the animal. If no one claimed it, the police would sell it and the proceeds would go to the following: 50% to the city treasury and 50% to the police department.

Keep your kitchen clean: In the 1800s, the city commission determined that unclean kitchens were not safe. Therefore, they determined it to be the duty of the Pensacola City Marshal and his officers to inspect every kitchen and premises within the city limits to ensure cleanliness. Failure to clean your kitchen would carry a $5 fine.

Bathing Naked: Without modern bathing facilities and bathrooms, people maintained personal hygiene differently from how they do it today. The most abundant supply of water came from Pensacola Bay. However, as the town became more inhabited, bathing in the bay was no longer an option. The city commission addressed the problem. On May 6, 1837, it enacted a new ordinance, "No person is allowed to bathe naked during the day in front of the city between Town Point (approx. 9th and Bayfront) and Bayou de la Aguada ('A' and Main Streets)."

Cant's: In 1837, the police were required to enforce the following:
- Shoot guns without asking the mayor first
- Run a horse or mule on the street or the sidewalk in the city limits
- Maim their animal in public
- Leave their cart, dray, or wagon in the street after dark
- Roll a barrel in the street or sidewalk in the city limits
- Fail to keep a 12 ft ladder in their yard
- Fail to have a well in their yard
- Have enough soot in their chimney to start a fire
- Water their horses in the public springs — the drinking supply for citizens

- Cut down the city's trees or the Market House
- Ring the City Bell if they were not the police
- Own or operate a gambling facility
- Have a store or business open on Sunday
- Store or sell any fruits or liquors from their house

The Arrest of John Wesley Hardin

Rumor has it that he shot a man for snoring too loudly. He claimed he killed 40 men "in self-defense." Research has shown that many of them were killed in cold blood. His name was John Wesley Hardin, and he was one of the most infamous and feared gunfighters in the history of the Old West. One of the men Hardin killed was Comanche County, Texas Deputy Charles Webb. An arrest warrant for Hardin was issued for murder. Hardin may have been deadly with a gun, but he was no match for the Texas Rangers, who were hot on his trail. He and his gang fled to Florida,

John Wesley Hardin

where it was quieter. Also, his partner, Robert Joshua "Brown" Bowen had family there. Bowen had his own troubles, being a robber and murderer in his own right — he had active warrants for murder and escape. Pensacola was 797 miles away from Comanche County, Texas. Sounded good.

Hardin and his gang settled in nearby north Santa Rosa county with the Neill Bowen family, northwest of a community that later became the town of Jay. "Life will be simpler now," he told himself. However, like many people, Hardin believed that the problem was the location. Not true. The problem was inside Hardin. Consequently, he continued in his habits. Under the alias "James W. Swain," he began hanging around in Pensacola, occasionally gambling and getting into scraps with others, but always under the radar. Mr. Swain was even familiar with Sheriff Hutchinson and Marshal Comyns.

Unbeknownst to Hardin or Bowen, the Texas Rangers, on the trail of Brown Bowen, had put an undercover Ranger on the case. Hardin's wife, Jane, was surveilled daily. They intercepted Bowen's mail and kept track of every person he contacted. One letter they intercepted revealed that the gang — including Hardin and Bowen — were living in Pensacola. Texas Rangers John Armstrong and Jack Duncan suddenly planned a road trip.

When William Chipley, superintendent of the Pensacola & Atlantic Railroad (and later mayor of Pensacola and Florida State Senator) learned that the Hardin gang was to catch a train at the Pensacola L&N Freight Depot, he accompanied the Rangers, Sheriff Hutchinson and Marshal Comyns to the train. A posse of Pensacola Police Officers and Escambia County Sheriff's Department Deputies were also on hand. Hutchinson, Duncan, Comyns and Chipley entered the train and apprehended Hardin before he could draw his weapon. However, one of his gang was fatally wounded in a shootout. Armstrong and Duncan escorted Hardin back to Texas where he stood trial. On June 5, 1878, John Wesley Hardin was sentenced to 25 years in state prison. He was released on February 17, 1894. On August 19, 1895, was shot in the back of the head by John Selman, Jr., killing him instantly.

The First Breathalyzer

There is a saying… "Advances in technology bring new challenges." The automobile is one of history's most significant breakthroughs in technology. However, with the introduction of automobiles came the need for red lights and traffic laws. Driving automobiles also introduces a new, dangerous problem: drunk drivers. In the past, there was never a need to determine if someone was driving under the influence, because there were no automobiles. So, no laws or punishment existed for driving drunk. With the advent of cars came the need to determine the amount of "drunkenness." The testing of drunk drivers began with a police officer arresting the driver based on his or her observations. Today, the intoxilyzer is the latest tool used.

"Police Take Guesswork out of Testing Alcohol." That was the title of a newspaper article written on January 20, 1958 about Pensacola's first Breathalyzer. Sgt. D.P. Caldwell, the instructor, gave an interview about how accurate the instrument was compared to the old drunkometer, which had been in use since 1931. It was a new and innovative tool invented by retired Indiana State Police Captain Robert F. Borkenstein for police departments to use. The instrument ushered in a new era of keeping the roads safe by stopping people who were driving drunk.

In the early 2000s, the author was visiting with Retired Chief Caldwell. As we talked about his days as a police officer, he suddenly stopped and said, "You have heard about the breathalyzer, haven't you?" The author explained that he knew what it was, but that the breathalyzer was replaced years ago by the intoxilyzer, which is the instrument of choice in the 2000s when a person is suspected of impaired driving. Chief Caldwell replied:

> *Well, you know, we used to use a Drunk-O-Meter. Some people called it a "Dial-a-drunk" because it was easy to manipulate. It was inaccurate, so something had to be developed to take its place. When I was the department's administrative sergeant, I had heard about a new instrument called a breathalyzer, and*

I thought it would be good if my department could get one. I contacted the inventor, a member of the Indiana State Police, and asked him if he could come to Pensacola to demonstrate it for us because we were interested in purchasing one. He agreed. The officer — I can't remember his name — arrived on the appointed evening at the San Carlos (Hotel) where the (Pensacola) Police Department had put him up. There was a lot of excitement. Visitors, dignitaries, media representatives, and police administrators were going to be there the next day. As soon as the officer arrived with the breathalyzer, he pulled me aside. 'I need your help!' he told me. 'This thing is brand new. I just built it and I know it works, but I have never tried it out! We need to try it out before the official demonstration tomorrow!"

Sergeant Caldwell, being a teetotaler, immediately found a willing volunteer to begin downing some free drinks to test the new instrument. So, in a room in the San Carlos Hotel at Palafox and Garden Streets, the very first breathalyzer test in history was performed. It performed wonderfully! The demonstration went off the next day "without a hitch" — according to D.P. Caldwell.

As it turns out, the January 20, 1958 edition of the *Pensacola News Journal* ran an article about the breathalyzer that paralleled what Chief Caldwell said. It stated: "The breathalyzer, which was perfected by Capt. Robert F. Borkenstein, director of the Indiana State Police Laboratory, is a semi-automatic colorimeter with photoelectric cells." Of course, the instrument was named incorrectly, and the technical description probably impressed some and confused others, but the article documented the test that paved the way for a more accurate instrument used in law enforcement.

The Dark Side

One of the saddest periods in the history of the Pensacola Police Department occurred during Chief Crosby Hall's tenure. The headlines of the December 8, 1960 edition of the Pensacola Journal read; "Owner's Records List 45 Cops in Pay Charges." Mrs. Lois Sheffield was the new owner of Sheffield's Garage. She took over the business after her husband, longtime owner Bill Sheffield died.

According to Mrs. Sheffield (and later corroborated by many officers), police officers received payoffs from Mr. Sheffield for bringing business his way. It worked like this: When a vehicle accident occurred within the city limits, it was (and still is) investigated by the Pensacola Police Department. Unless a driver requested another wrecker service, most officers either recommended Sheffield's or simply called on the radio for the company to respond. A small percentage of the fee would be paid to the officer. Of course, this is illegal, and Mrs. Sheffield hated the practice, although her husband ran it, and it brought in a lot of money for her family.

After her husband's death, Lois Sheffield stopped the practice of these payments to officers. Of course, officers — many of whom did not know the action was illegal — were unhappy, and they let Lois know about it. There was talk that some made threats to her. Because the practice continued and payments were demanded by officers, Lois went to the Pensacola Police Department superiors. But the administration did nothing. Frustrated, Lois brought records to the local AAA motor club and the media. The records showed payoffs listed to officers from February 1959–April 1960, when her husband died. After that, she claimed that the officers pressured her to resume the $10 payoffs for business sent her way during crash investigations. As it turned out, 17 officers were charged, two were acquitted, and 15 cases were dropped.

Then, while the Department was still trying to recover after the wrecker scandal, things got worse. In April of 1961, eight Pensacola police officers and two Escambia County Deputies were arrested for taking part in a burglary ring. According to an interview with a fellow officer: an officer would approach a business, break out a window, take a television, put it in the trunk of his car and call in a burglary. Another common practice occurred when an officer, at the scene of a legitimate burglary, was offered property by the business owner, who would then include it in the stolen items list. Of the eight officers charged, three served time in prison, one received probation (off the force), and three were acquitted. The eighth, John Trevathan, disappeared and was never heard from again. Most employees who were working at the time of the scandals, all agree that many other officers were involved in both events but were never caught or charged.

Officer Marion Cotita

Officer Dean Trimble

Pensacola's Connection to the JFK Murder

We have all heard the story: President John F. Kennedy, our 35th U. S. President, was sitting in the rear of a convertible, touring downtown Dallas on November 22, 1963. As he turned into Dealey Plaza, Lee Harvey Oswald pointed a rifle at him from the Texas schoolbook depository and fired the shots that ended his life. Then, after Oswald was charged, he was killed by Jack Ruby, the local night-club owner, who was such a patriot that he shot Oswald out of hate. The end. Period. Maybe...

Follow-up investigations rubber stamped the original reports. Then came the questions about Cuba's involvement, the FBI, the vice president, the CIA, and the military. More questions followed about the local police, the mob, Cuban exiles, and New Orleans. Inquiries about combinations of these entities were raised. Documentaries and scientific recreations conclude that the murder could not have occurred the way it was originally supported. People began to ask, "Could the assassination have been a plot born from a conspiracy?" The overwhelming answer was "Yes, hundreds of them." Further, there were the fringe reports. One guy knew someone that knew someone that was related to Oswald, and then he died. The Warren commission, a panel brought together to investigate what happened, concluded that it was a straight-forward, no-nonsense, Oswald murder.

Then came technology. When re-creations and sound bites and eyewitness testimony are put together, the results conclude that Oswald could not acted alone. Finally, the television shows came out. The movie "JFK" led the crowd. People began to reconsider what might have happened. Many theories still abound, and many have very plausible possibilities.

Hank Killam, a Pensacola boy, often found himself in trouble growing up — in school, the neighborhood and in his family. As a teenager, his troubles increased and often involved the police. Thefts, burglaries, fights, etc. are examples of his regular trips to the police station. Hank was big — he stood over 6 feet tall and weighed over 200 lbs. He was also a good-looking kid, but he had trouble abiding by the law. When he was put on probation for a business burglary, he couldn't follow the rules, and absconded to Dallas, Texas, where he lived about five years. He met and married Wanda Davis. Wanda was a cigarette girl, dancer, and stripper in a club — a club owned by Jack Ruby. For a while, Hank even worked as a bouncer for Jack. Hank also sought out and befriended John Carter, a house painter for work. John hired Hank to work for him. John lived in the same boarding house as Lee Harvey Oswald. John also knew Wanda and the three of them (Wanda, John, and Hank) often talked together, maybe about things they shouldn't be talking about, at Jack Ruby's club, the *Carousel Lounge.*

On the day of the president's assassination and the capture of Oswald — November 22, 1963 — Hank came home from work, pale and shocked, Wanda recalled. She figured he was stunned that his president had been assassinated in his town. Of course, he was shocked. Everyone was shocked. But…was it more? Wanda said that Hank stayed glued to the television that night, watching the latest reports. He became more and more agitated and paranoid. Investigators from different departments — both local and federal — sought him out constantly. He complained that "plotters" wanted to speak with him and kept harassing him. Wanda was certain he was afraid of something. She was convinced that something sinister — related to the assassination — was at work. Suddenly, a few months after the assassination of the president, Hank informed Wanda that he had to leave Dallas. He moved 1138 miles away — to Tampa, Florida. He began selling cars there. However, he made the mistake of talking too much about his destination, and "agents and plotters" (as Hank referred to them) soon drew the information from Wanda. They found him in his new job and began "hounding" him again. From place to place he went, trying without success to keep a job in one spot, becoming more mistrustful of everyone. In March 1964, he couldn't stay in Tampa any longer. Even though he felt certain that a warrant existed for his arrest, he decided to return to his childhood town — Pensacola.

On March 15, 1964, Hank arrived in Pensacola. He went to the home of his mother, Mary Killam, at 316 W. Romana Street. As they were talking, he told her that he was frightened about what might happen to him. Soon he contacted his old friends and got caught up about old times. While speaking with his brother Earl about the JFK situation, he said "I'm a dead man, but I've run as far as I'm going to run." He let Earl know that his concerns stemmed from not being able to escape the long fingers associated with the JFK ordeal. Hank stayed with his mother — for two days.

On March 16, Hank got a letter in the mail. He read it, and a deathly fear came over his face. He kept mentioning that he was afraid. His mother didn't know what he meant, nor did she want to. That evening, his paranoia rose to the point that he began talking to himself and walking around in the house and yard. At 1:35 on the morning of the 17th, Mary, desperate for some help, called the police. Pensacola Police Officer Henry Reeves responded, along with others. One of the other officers remarked, "It's just Hank. Don't worry about it." Hank had worked as an informant for the PPD before, so they apparently didn't think he would be in danger. Mary told Officer Reeves that Hank had had mental problems and that he had been having black-out spells recently. She had an appointment later in the day for him to see a psychiatrist. Reeves tried to convince Mrs. Killam to take Hank to the emergency room, but she resisted, promising to take him to the doctor later that day. Officer Reeves, knowing Hank, then talked him into going to bed and getting some sleep. Hank obeyed. Officer Reeves instructed Mary to sit outside his door to ensure he did not leave. She agreed and Reeves left.

Around 3 am, the telephone rang, waking Hank and Mary. Hank talked for a few seconds and hung up. Mary went back to sleep in the chair outside her son's room. A few minutes later she woke up when she heard a car door slam and a vehicle drive away. She thought it was strange, because the Killams didn't own a car. Suddenly, a strange, cold feeling came over Mary. It got worse when she discovered that Hank was gone. At 3:40, she called the police again, worried because Hank had not returned. Officer Reeves again responded. As Reeves searched for Hank, he got a call about a body lying in a pool of blood on the sidewalk on the Northwest corner of Palafox and Intendencia — just four blocks from the Killam home.

The view that Officer Henry Reeves found when he arrived was gruesome. The huge plate-glass window of *The Linen Store*, 125 S. Palafox Street was shattered, and glass was lying everywhere. Inside the store were bloody footprints, marking as far back as six feet from the broken window. All of that paled in comparison to what was in the middle of the sidewalk, thirty-five feet from the window. There lay Hank Killam in a pool of his own blood with his throat cut. Reeves called for an ambulance and Hank was taken to Escambia General Hospital, where he was pronounced dead. At first, the police ruled the death a suicide, while the coroner's office ruled it an accident. When they were questioned, one officer said that they were told to "shut it down" and not talk about it anymore. No autopsy was ordered or conducted.

On February 22, 2019, the author interviewed Elton Killam. For many years, Elton practiced law in Pensacola. He is also a cousin to Hank Killam. Not satisfied with the shallow investigation that the Pensacola Police Department had conducted, he made numerous contacts, conducted interviews, read books, and watched movies to find the truth. He explained the situation to the author about his cousin's death.

The Warren Commission, the JFK movie, other investigations, movies, television shows, books and articles have been written about JFK's assassination. Many people have said that they have finally found the answer…but no answer has been found yet. Also, rumors abound about the number of witnesses to the JFK assassination who had a similar end to Hank Killam. The numbers range from fifteen to more than one hundred. No one knows, or has ever proven, that the deaths are connected, but it appears that Hank Killam's death might have been one.

Murder for Hire

For 17 years, they worked together. They were friends — close, as cops often are. That is why Sgt. Lucien Mitchell was surprised when his buddy, Sgt. Isaac Halford came to him one day at police headquarters and offered him money to "take care of someone." Mitchell asked Halford what he meant by "take care of someone," to which Halford replied, "by killing them." Mitchell was no stranger to tough situations. After all, he had been a cop for a long time. In addition, Lucien had that kind of reputation. Many people commented "Wow! I would have come to him also. If anyone could kill someone, Lucien could!" After all, he had been in some scrapes before. Legend had it that Lucien put a notch on his gun handle every time he killed a man. So far, there were six, but they were all legal. But to murder an innocent woman in cold blood — he didn't want anything to do with that. Lucien did not answer right away. He knew he would have no part in the murder of an innocent woman, but he contemplated what to do.

Sergeant Lucien Mitchell

Jim and Gerry Naes lived what appeared to be very comfortable and successful lives. They had three children, lived in an upper-middle-class neighborhood and both drove nice cars. Jim had a good business that provided the family with the means to live a somewhat extravagant lifestyle, which often landed them on the society page of the local news. However, the home was not a happy one. Their divorce was final on January 9, 1974. The judge's decision left Gerry with custody of the children, the house, child support, alimony, and a lump sum of $20,000. This did not sit well with Jim at all. After all, he was used to getting his way. He had worked hard for his money, and now he felt he should be reaping the benefits of his labor. He checked with his lawyer — he couldn't change the judge's mind or "overrule" his decision. There was, however, something that he could do. He contacted his friend, Pensacola Police Sergeant Isaac Halford, and offered to pay him $5000 to murder Gerry, who in turn contacted Sergeant Mitchell and made the offer to him.

Lucien listened. Inside, he was shocked. He didn't say anything at first. Instead, he reported the incident to State Attorney Curtis Golden. Everything that Lucien did after that was part of an investigation under the supervision of Golden. First, while being recorded, he contacted Halford and got the contact information. The recorded telephone call was made to Mr. Naes, who agreed to meet Lucien at #212, Wellington Arms apartments. Lucien showed up in plain clothes, wearing a wire. Jim Naes gave Lucien $2500 and promised him another $2500 upon completion of the task. After the transaction, on April 30, 1975, Lucien met with Halford and gave him $500 in marked bills as bonus money for setting the job up, which Halford pocketed. A few minutes after the meeting, Halford, who had gone to the Escambia County courthouse on other business, was approached by two of his fellow officers — Perry Knowles and Mike Thompson. To his surprise, they placed him under arrest for conspiracy to commit murder. Meanwhile, Jim Naes left town on a business trip to Alabama.

Sergeant Isaac Halford

When a person is arrested on a warrant from another state, he is taken to the nearest jail and held there until a hearing can be arranged to see a judge — usually the next day. If the person refuses to waive extradition to the state that wants him, he must remain in jail until a Governor's Warrant is applied for. The extradition can take three months. So, when Jim Naes was contacted and informed that a warrant existed for his arrest for conspiracy to commit murder, he agreed to return to Pensacola and turn himself in, which he did. Both men eventually made bond — Jim for $50,000 and Halford for $10,000.

While Jim was out on bond, the Pensacola Police Department provided round-the-clock security for Gerry and the kids, even though the residence was out of their jurisdiction, in Escambia County. With protection from harm and the realization that the case was set for trial, Gerry Naes was safe. From all indications, she would be able to live and to raise her children in the same relative manner as before the incident, but with one exception. With Jim in prison, there would be no financial support from him. He would not be able to pay child support or alimony. Gerry would have to raise three children and earn her own income. It was overwhelming. However, instead of a lengthy prison sentence, if Jim were sentenced to probation, he could continue working and help with the finances. So, Gerry found herself arguing for leniency for the husband who betrayed her and paid to have her killed. When the situation was presented to the judge, he understood and sentenced Jim to probation. As soon as the case was settled, however, Jim fled to St. Louis and remained there. Gerry never saw any support. Life is full of irony.

The Deadly Train Derailment

The Thorshov family lived in an area called Gull Point, which overlooked the Escambia Bay to the east and provided an elevated view of the CSX railroad tracks that meandered along the water's edge. On the evening of Wednesday, November 9, 1977, the Thorshovs were relaxing at their home when they suddenly heard a loud crash — the dreaded, unmistakable crash of a train derailment.

It was normal for trains to come along the tracks near the Thorshov home, as they passed by several times a day. On this day, however, a train consisting of two SD-45 locomotives and 35 cars derailed at 6:09 pm, spilling its cargo all along the bluffs. Some of the cargo contained anhydrous ammonia, a toxic chemical whose deadly vapor permeated the entire neighborhood known as Gull Point.

Dr. Thorsov, a local pathologist, and his family were rushed to the hospital and treated for exposure to the deadly fumes. According to the Centers for Disease Control website, anhydrous ammonia is a colorless gas or liquid with a pungent, suffocating odor whose symptoms cause irritation to the eyes, nose, and throat. It causes breathing difficulty, wheezing, chest pain, pulmonary edema, pink frothy sputum; skin burns, vesiculation and liquid frostbite. Dr. Thorshov died that night at the hospital of suffocation from his injuries.

Pensacola Police Officers suddenly had to evacuate 600 area residents from Interstate10 to Langley Avenue, and from Spanish Trail to Escambia Bay — about 2 square miles, while battling a deadly fog. Meanwhile, 500 residents from south Santa Rosa County were evacuated because the toxic cloud of anhydrous ammonia gas floated east over the bay and toward the Garcon Point area. While many people commented on the dangers that the residents were exposed to, most people did not consider that the officers voluntarily went into the toxic area to rescue others.

The first indication came from an emergency phone call to Dispatcher Jerry Potts. A resident in the area heard a loud crashing sound and he knew that he heard a train derailment. Other calls reported a cloud over the highway. Officers were immediately dispatched to respond and investigate.

Officer Scott Pelham, the first officer on the scene, was patrolling in that area when he received the first call about an explosion, and he described a frightening scene. Not knowing what the situation was, he responded with his lights and siren. As soon as he arrived, he knew it was a train crash and realized the danger of being in the area. He backed out and turned around, checking on homeowners as he left. As it turned out, that decision probably saved his life — or at least a hospital stay. Less than a mile down the road from where he stopped a deadly toxic cloud hovered over the road.

The derailment came close to home for Investigator Wes Cummings. Driving home from work, Wes passed through the intersection of Creighton Road and Scenic Highway that became deadly 10 minutes later. He heard a call on the radio of possible smoke at the intersection he had just passed through. Before the night was over, his next-door neighbor was exposed and had to be taken to the hospital.

Officer Bill Chavers was also working that night. When dispatched, he responded. "I almost drove into the clouded area. Later I was assigned the task of driving out to the little point area at the end of Creighton to check the small group of homes. It was like the movie *Andromeda* (warring against uncivilized chaos). The fire department provided an air pack for me to use. The homes were abandoned, doors open, food on tables, TVs on, everything laying out because the people had immediately fled the area. It was scary and weird."

Rookie Officer Greg Moody responded to the explosion as well. Without much training or experience, common sense told him it was a bad idea to drive through the huge white fog that hung over the highway. He turned around and spent the rest of the time assisting residents out of the area and directing traffic.

Officer Lamar Pate recalled that night well. He was patrolling the west side of town with Officer Sammy Mayo — two to a car. Since all available officers were needed at the site of the derailment on the east side, Officers Mayo and Pate managed all calls for half of the city of Pensacola.

Within minutes the disaster was widespread. Some officers were called in to work, and the relaxing night they were expecting never happened. The initial phone calls to the police department were followed by thousands from across the globe. Worried residents called to see if the cloud would float in their direction, members of the media wanted more information, and out-of-town friends and relatives called to find out about loved ones who might have been affected. The dispatchers and desk sergeant were an addition to handle the overwhelming radio and telephone traffic.

Emergency shelters were set up at Bayview Community Center and two local churches. Three shelters were set up in Santa Rosa county. At least 18 people were taken to area hospitals. While the highest number of victims was taken to West Florida Hospital, Sacred Heart took in the most severe, the Thorshov family. Besides the death of Dr. Thorshov, his wife and two children were admitted, listed as critical the first night.

In the aftermath, city and county leaders were angry over the seemingly lack of concern that L&N Railroad officials had for the disaster. According to the *Pensacola News Journal*, derailments had occurred in West Florida in the past 30 months, many of them containing toxic materials. Discussions took place to ban all toxic chemicals into Pensacola. While many councilmen and commissioners talked with the media, Commissioners Kenneth Kelson and Marvin Beck were at the scene as quickly as they could get there.

The empty houses became easy targets for looters. In the evacuated areas, residents were prevented from going home anywhere from 24 hours to several days, depending on the distance between the homes and the fumes. Lieutenant Mike Maney recalled that he and several other officers were assigned to patrol the off-limits areas for a few days for unauthorized persons.

Sergeant Skip Bollens was there and told this story: "I had finished work for the day and was called back to work traffic control at Scenic and Langley. A newsman kept insisting he had to go North on scenic (toward the crash scene). He refused to turn around or go South. I finally indicated East (dead end toward the bay, not the crash) and he took off 10–18 (in a hurry). As he arrived in full speed at the dead end, he slammed on his brakes. I thought he was going to slide all the way to the railroad tracks that made their way past the dead end! He finally left, telling me what he thought of me. I was relieved in time to go to Red Cross van for coffee and a hot dog before heading back to work for the next day. I was at the Incident Command when the national news cornered Sergeant (Elmer) Powell for a news release. Cameras rolling, live feed, they asked what had happened. The salty sergeant stated in a slow, southern drawl, "The train fell off the track." Irritated, they stopped the live cameras and backed off until releases were made.

On Sunday, January 22, 1978. 74 days following the disaster, another tragedy struck. Mrs. Lloyda Thorshov succumbed to the injuries that she had suffered from the derailment, leaving her two children without either parent. The official cause was listed as respiratory failure. A lawsuit against L & N brought about sweeping changes, not only to the tracks along Pensacola's scenic bluffs, but also to the entire railroad industry, bringing about much needed improvements and safety measures. Laws were changed, making rail travel safer. It is a blessing to see the community join to help in times of disaster. The railroad incident was no exception.

As sad as the event was, had it not been for the courageous acts of the officers of the Pensacola Police Department, the firefighters of the Pensacola Fire Department, neighbors and citizens, the death toll would have been much higher.

The Capture of Ted Bundy

Working the graveyard shift is…different. Sometimes it's slow, sometimes it's crazy, and sometimes it's — creepy. When the world is winding down, midnight shift workers are just beginning. Some police officers like it while others hate it. There are a few advantages to working the midnight shift. The streets are usually less busy, the officers are usually less busy, and the heavy brass of the department is not at work, making for less tension. However, a common statement by officers is, "If you get into something on midnights, it's really big!"

1:30 AM on Wednesday, February 15, 1978 was a quiet time for David Lee. Officer Lee was a Pensacola Police Officer, working the midnight shift on the west side of Pensacola. Two of the qualities of a good beat officer are to know the people and businesses on his beat and to protect them like a guard dog. That is what Officer Lee did. As he usually did when working midnights, Officer Lee was checking the buildings on his beat, his main objective to prevent and foil burglaries.

Old friends met there. It was that kind of place — when you walked in, you probably knew somebody, or felt like you did. Most people loved eating at Oscar's Restaurant. When it was open, the parking lot was usually full. And it was not unusual to find one of Pensacola's Finest eating there. It

Sign in front of Oscar's Restaurant

was a Pensacola icon. Located in an old building in a less-than-affluent area of town, Oscar's had that special charm that drew people to it. It felt... familiar.

David Lee drove his patrol car slowly through back streets, along Cervantes Street and between businesses. He used his spotlight to better see that neighborhoods and businesses were safe. As he eased his cruiser behind Oscar's Restaurant, 2805 West Cervantes Street, he saw a beige Volkswagen Beetle slowly making its way through the parking lot. This sight attracted David's attention. Like all good beat cops, he knew the employees at Oscars and what they drove. *Strange*, he thought to himself. "Nobody that works here drives a VW. He tried to think of scenarios that would cause such a sight. He considered driving off, but the guard dog in him convinced him to go back, so he decided to check it out. Just then, the vehicle suddenly fled from the parking lot. As Officer Lee followed it, he called in his situation on the radio, checking the tag. It came back as a stolen vehicle belonging to Kenneth Misner from Tallahassee. This transmission attracted the attention of other officers, who headed toward David.

Officer Lee prepared to stop it and possibly find out why the driver was cruising in his town behind Oscar's Restaurant. However, the Volkswagen sped up in an obvious attempt to elude David. Finally, he stopped the Volkswagen a mile and a half up the road. He pulled it over outside the city limits at "W" and Cross streets near Catholic High School. David didn't know what he had. He did know that he was approaching the driver of a car parked behind a closed business (in HIS area of town), and that the vehicle fled when he approached it. Not taking any chances, he ordered the driver out of the car and made him lie down. When Lee approached, the man kicked Lee's legs from under him and a fight ensued. Finally, the man broke free and ran northeast into the neighborhood. Lee chased the man through the area, finally firing two shots. As he approached the suspect, he attacked Lee, and another fight began, but this time over the gun. Lee and responding officers finally subdued the man and placed him in cuffs. He was taken to jail. A search of the man's possessions and of the contents of the car revealed several documents, including many credit cards in the name of Kenneth Misner, the owner of the stolen car. Things didn't add up, David Lee asked himself. Why would a man be driving his own stolen car?

Detective Norman Chapman lived 40 miles from the police station, near the small town of Jay, Florida. He lived out in the country, and his accent and mannerisms reflected his laid-back country life. When Norman got out of the U. S. Army, he decided to become a Pensacola Police Officer. Soon, he was transferred to Investigations as a detective. In the early morning hours of February 15, Norman's phone rang.

"Sorry to wake you detective, but you need to come in. Officer Lee stopped a vehicle that is listed as stolen out of Tallahassee. We have the driver in custody."

Rubbing the sleep from his eyes, Norman began the business of getting dressed and heading out. Detectives make a habit of having clothing and equipment laid out — just in case they are called into work during the night. When Detective Chapman arrived, he met the man…who claimed that he was Kenneth Misner. The man was not used to Norman's slow, southern drawl, but he liked him. The man made the mistake of believing the stereotype of a southern country boy being dimwitted and backward. Chapman interviewed the man and immediately made a connection with him. Chapman sensed there was something different about this man who called himself Kenneth Misner, something unusual that the man was hiding. Chapman established — not a friendship — but a relationship with the man which would last for many years. The man was very personable and extremely intelligent. However, he was proud of himself.

His pride was the element that Detective Chapman focused on. In an almost Gomer Pyle manner, Norman acted as if he was fascinated with the man's intelligence. As he freely spoke with the man, something wasn't right. He had just been arrested in a stolen car with stolen items, fled from the police, then tried to take an officer's weapon. Yet he appeared relaxed and smooth. He was personable — almost charming. How would a man of his intelligence and ability find himself in this situation? It didn't feel right. The man was fingerprinted, and his prints were sent to the Federal Bureau of Investigation. After a period, the FBI identified the man through his fingerprints. His name was Theodore Robert Bundy.

Ted Bundy's name had been in the papers and on television across the United States. He was last seen in the northwest where he escaped and fled. He was on the FBI's *Ten Most-Wanted List*. The infamous serial murderer and escape artist had disappeared from the Glenwood Springs, CO Jail and resurfaced in Pensacola. During the hours that Chapman interviewed Bundy, he made statements that proved significant in the case of Kimberly Leach, a 12-year-old girl who was murdered in Lake City and buried in a shallow grave nearby. Bundy was found guilty of this crime and sentenced to die in the electric chair.

Ted Bundy

The information which Bundy related to Detective Chapman was important to the case. As Bundy's date with electric chair "Old Sparky" neared, he requested that Chapman — now the chief of police — come to visit him on death row. Chief Chapman knew that Bundy wanted to tell where more bodies were buried. It was obvious that Bundy wanted to extend his life by having additional charges brought against him, therefore postponing his execution. Chapman refused to see Bundy, who was put to death on January 24, 1989.

Donna in the Bay

"They have lost an airliner from the radar…It just disappeared…This is not good." Pensacola Police Officer Jim Simmons said to his family as he hung up the phone. Jim, the author's father, was one of the police officers assigned to the Pensacola Regional Airport. He had been at work at the airport that day, May 8, 1978, and had only been home a few hours. Just after 9 pm that night, he got a phone call from the airport dispatcher informing him that the FAA officials in the tower had lost a National Airlines 727 jetliner they were tracking. The airliner had lined up to approach the runway from the east, right over Escambia Bay and Scenic Highway. As it came close to the bay, it disappeared from the radar.

The wreckage from the National Airlines craft in Escambia Bay

The weather was foggy that night — very foggy. Earlier that night, the FAA officials had just diverted an Eastern Airlines plane to Mobile because of the dense fog. The next plane to approach was National Airlines Flight 193, and it dropped from radar as it was approaching. Jim explained that the disappearance of the plane most often means the plane dropped below the altitude that can be picked up on the radar. He said that the plane must have simply dropped too low over the water, but that was not likely — all indications were that it had crashed. As he said, it was not good. He got dressed and returned to the airport. It was going to be a long night.

Almost immediately, the phone calls started coming into the police emergency line about an airplane in Escambia Bay. The jet, a Boeing 727, had 58 reported souls onboard. At that time, National Airlines had a policy that every airplane had a name which was written on the side of the aircraft. This one was named Donna. Officer Scott Pelham was the first officer on the scene. Six months earlier, he had been the first officer on the scene of the L & N derailment. Due to the limited information he had upon arrival, he could only keep a lookout for debris and survivors. He felt helpless.

A huge advantage to landing in the bay is the possibility for a soft landing. As a result, no one died during the crash landing. However, many problems occur when a plane crashes into a body of water at night. No one — passengers, families, airport officials, or crew members — knew where the plane landed. They did not know if it was in one piece or thousands. Rescue was difficult — it took boats to get people out. It was dark, so people were unable to see the plane. Not a good situation.

At the Pensacola Regional Airport, loved ones who were there to greet the passengers waited for word on the plane. At first, they thought it might be late. But then they could tell that there was a problem. Between the airline employees, airport officials and police scurrying about in an unusual manner, they soon sensed something bad had happened. Eventually, they were told that it appeared the plane had crashed. Reactions ranged from calm to weepy to hysterical.

As is often the case in emergencies, the best and the worst come out in people. The jet had crashed into Escambia Bay in 9–12 ft of water close to Garcon Point in Santa Rosa county. A boat and barge that happened to be nearby approached the airliner, tied up to it, and began rescuing passengers. Fishing boats, pleasure craft, and law enforcement boats all came to the rescue. Interestingly, one nearby crab fisherman continued to check his crab traps, seemingly unaffected by the tragedy.

Scenic Highway, which overlooks the bay at the point adjacent to the crash scene, quickly became full of spectators. On each side of the road, cars pulled off, and people gathered to catch a glimpse. The crowd grew to a point that traffic became yet another problem. All Pensacola Police traffic officers were called out and responded on motorcycles — not for the crash, but because of rubberneckers' vehicles blocking traffic. Sergeant Rick Buddin recalls that he was called by his supervisor and ordered to get into uniform and report for work immediately. The job of handling traffic was as hectic as the rescue efforts.

When the plane first crashed, the interior lights blinked and went out. Salt water mixed with jet fuel began pouring in the passenger cabin, causing panic. The flight attendants kept people as calm as possible, but that task was a difficult one. Most people tried to help each other escape. A 2-year-old boy was crying but was passed from one passenger to another until he was out of danger, on a wing under the care of a male passenger. Sadly, his mother wasn't aware of his rescue, and drowned trying to locate him. Amazingly, out of 58 passengers and crew members, only three died of drowning. Many people had injuries from exposure, burns, bruises, internal injuries, ingestion of jet fuel, and shock, but 55 of 58 recovered.

As with any disaster situation, there was some confusion. There was no command post at Garcon Point, the closest land to the scene. It was set up at the east end of the Escambia Bay Bridge, which was closer to hospitals and emergency equipment. However, as some of the passengers were rescued, they were taken to the nearest land and dropped off, leaving them unaccounted for by the officials. As a result, first responders went to both sides of the bay — Escambia and Santa Rosa counties. Officer Mike Maney was off duty at home when he heard about the crash. He proceeded to the command post to help. He and Officer Clayton Ard walked the beach on the Santa Rosa side searching for survivors, debris, etc. for several hours, but found nothing. At the time, the condition of the plane and passengers was unknown. Detective Wes Cummings was working on a stakeout when he heard of the disaster on the police radio. He drove to the closest intersection to the crash. After meeting with Chief of Police James Davis, he conducted foot recon along the shore on the West side of the bay for survivors or pieces of airplane, but to no avail.

It was unclear for a long time how the crash happened. The airport's runway that was equipped with instrument landing equipment was out of operation, causing the landing to occur from the direction of Escambia Bay — by sight.

On June 29, Pilot George Kunz testified before investigators with the National Transportation Safety Board that he was reading 1300–1400 feet on his altimeter while the actual reading was 300–400 feet. So, as he began his descent, he contacted the water. Kunz, the co-pilot, and the navigator were all fired from National Airlines, who began working to settle the many lawsuits that came from the incident.

The Black Widow

"He's a lucky man…God's been with him." Those were the words of Albert Gentry, brother of John Gentry. Albert was referring to John's two close calls with death. When John was serving in the military in the Vietnam War, he stepped on a mine while on patrol. The mine exploded under him causing severe injuries and a lengthy hospital stay, but no permanent injury. Then, on Wednesday night, June 25, 1983, John's car exploded when he turned on the ignition in downtown Pensacola.

John Gentry was a wallpaper businessman from Pensacola. In 1983, John met a woman named Judi Buenoano, a nurse who lived in the nearby town of Gulf Breeze. Despite her nursing qualifications, Judi owned and operated a nail sculpturing salon. She was a successful businesswoman from all appearances of her lifestyle.

Detective Ted Chamberlain

Ted Chamberlain was born on July 21, 1945, in the historic town of Attleboro, Massachusetts. Both his grandfather and his father had been police officers, so Ted was destined to follow in their footsteps. Right out of high school, Ted joined the U.S. Army and was sent straight to Vietnam to fight in the war. After he got out of the Army, he returned to Massachusetts and joined the "family business" of law enforcement, becoming an officer in his hometown. In 1976, Ted became a Pensacola Police Officer. Ted retired in 2013, ending his

37-year career. During that time, he served in patrol, the Tactical unit (his favorite), and Investigations. Ted was the kind of officer who very much liked working with the guys. An amateur race-car driver, he always drove with the windows down and one foot on the gas and the other on the brake.

After the explosion, it didn't take long to suspect foul play. Someone had deliberately set a bomb in the car. In the middle of the night, the phones of Detectives Rick Steele and Ted Chamberlain rang. In a 2019 interview with Ted, he said that he first suspected Judi when he arrived at the scene. Ted recalled "Instead of parking near the restaurant, she parked her corvette a long way off — why? After the initial incident, Ted interviewed Judi a few days later. Her arrogance bothered him. "She bragged that she earned $500,000 per year." He later found out that the life insurance Judi took out on Gentry was for $500,000. One of the first crucial tasks in detective work is to check the players' backgrounds. In the Pensacola Police Department's Records section, he searched for Judias Buenoano. Nothing. Ted had a sudden thought. A young Hispanic woman worked in the Records section, so Ted asked her "What does the name *Buenoano* mean in English?" "It means *Goodyear*" she answered. Bingo! Ted found several death investigations that involved Judi's husbands, boyfriends and even her son. The locations ranged from Pensacola to Colorado, and insurance money had a hand in every one of them.

Judi Buenoano, The Black Widow

Detectives Steele and Chamberlain worked the case, eventually developing Judi as a primary suspect. Further investigation revealed that Judi had previously tried to kill Gentry by using poison. To improve his health, she began giving him a regiment of "Vitamin C" that would make feel better and be healthier, she told him. A task force involving investigators from all interested agencies was formed. Soon, more of the task force members began suspecting Judi in the death of her son, her husband, her common-law husband, and perhaps one or two more people. Each person had a life insurance policy paid to…Judi Buenoano.

After a long and exhausting trial, Judi Buenoano was, on March 31, 1984, convicted of pre-meditated first-degree murder in the death of her son, who drowned while on a canoe trip with Judy in the East River. She was given a life sentence. She was also convicted of the attempted murder of John Gentry and received a 12-year prison sentence for it. Because of the work of Steele, Chamberlain, members of the task force, and especially of State Attorney Russ Edgar, Judi was convicted of premeditated first-degree murder in the death of her husband, James Goodyear, in Orlando in 1971. She received the death penalty and met her fate on Monday, March 30, 1998.

Pensacola Police's Talking Car

"That's it! Just like Herbie!" Pensacola Police Officer Mack Cramer was sitting in a crime prevention seminar in Tampa when he heard about a "theme car" idea. It came to him — he could acquire a theme car for the Pensacola Police. And it could have eyes with eyelashes and would talk and make noises, remotely. And it would be painted like the other police cars, but it could talk to the kids!

As soon as Mack returned to Pensacola, he called the other officers in his section, Community Relations, together and shared the idea with them. They loved it! A sketch was made of a Volkswagen Beetle painted like a Pensacola Police Car. On November 18, 1981, *News Journal* Writer Cindy West published an article. The title above the sketch read "Pensacola Police need a Name for their Baby." The caption on the picture said, "Hey Kids, Give

Blinky the Talking Car

Me a Name: Name the Car Contest." The car, equipment, electronics, paint job, and blue lights were all donated, as was the bicycle to be awarded to the child that suggested the winning name for the car. In addition, the Police Explorers provided the labor to prepare the car for painting and equipping. On January 16, after sifting through over 3000 entries for a name for the Pensacola Police Department's 2300 lb. baby, Tracy Franz was announced as the winner. She received a brand-new Huffy bicycle donated by TG&Y.

For the next 30 years, Blinky continued to amaze kids. Many found it astonishing that a car with eyelashes could talk to you and answer your questions! Many children, now adults, fondly remember Blinky, the police department's talking baby.

Pensacola's Axe Murderer

Ramon Grayson never fit in. His family had moved to Federal Way, Washington, in 1975 when Ramon was 10 years old. Five years later he had begun experimenting with drugs. He attended a couple of high schools, but still didn't fit.

A quiet, loner type, Ramon's demeanor changed drastically when he was 19. When he flew into a rage and threatened to kill his mother and father, they had to do something. Maybe a change of scenery and friends would help. Mr. Grayson's mother, Willie Mae Grayson, agreed to let him stay with her. So, Ramon packed up and went to Pensacola to live at 2306 N. 6th Avenue to live with his grandmother.

Ramon Grayson

Willie Mae Grayson worked hard and was a dependable employee in the cafeteria at Warrington Middle School. She led a quiet life on North Sixth Avenue with her boarder, Timothy Mitchell, and Freeway, the pet German Shepherd. The home was in a typical middle-class neighborhood with a park a block away. It was the perfect grandma's house.

As soon as Ramon arrived in Pensacola in early February 1984, things took a turn for the worse. Willie begged Ramon to enroll at Booker T. Washington High School. Even though he was a sensitive boy, he didn't seem to want to get close to his grandmother. Six weeks later, Ramon was suspended from school for smoking.

On Thursday morning, March 22, 1984, the employees at the Warrington Middle School cafeteria began wondering where Willie Mae was. After all, she was always there, and never missed a day. So, they called the Pensacola Police. Carlos Padilla was the first officer to respond.

Officer Padilla was a young, handsome Hispanic officer. It was said that when Carlos passed a group of ladies, their collective breath was taken away. But Carlos was not just good-looking, he was also smart. As soon as he arrived, he sensed there was something wrong. The front gate had a "BEWARE OF DOG" sign on it — but no dog. Carlos even rattled the gate to attract the dog's attention. Nothing. *Hmmm, Strange* he thought. Warily, he opened the gate, made his way to the front door, and knocked. No answer. Carlos looked in a window but saw nothing. Should he kick the door in to check on Willie Mae's welfare? Her action of not showing up was so out-of-the-ordinary that it prompted a call from her co-workers. Or should he simply just leave? After all, there was no indication of foul play. Puzzled, he called his supervisor, Henry Cassady.

Officer Carlos Padilla

Sgt. Cassady was a veteran who had seen it all — or almost. When he arrived, Carlos relayed the situation to him. Together, they went around the house, checked the car, searched the yard, and looked in windows for anything suspicious. Finally, through one of the bedroom windows, they noticed blood on the bed. That was enough. The officers, concluding that someone may need help, kicked the door in. No one answered the announcement

"Police" that was made, and the living room looked normal. When they got to the dining room door, though, a grisly view awaited them. The hacked up and obviously dead bodies of Mrs. Grayson, Mr. Mitchell, and Freeway lay on the floor. The two officers, realizing they had just entered a crime scene, backed out and called for Crime Scene detectives to respond and begin processing.

Detective John Hollingsworth was assigned the case and immediately began canvassing the neighborhood. A neighbor said that she and her daughter were walking home from the store when, as they passed the house around 7:30 PM, they heard screams. Startled and concerned for their neighbor, they listened for anything further, but heard nothing. Dismissing the noise, they continued on their way, not realizing that they had just "earwitnessed" a murder. The neighbor added that she went into her house. Soon after, she saw a young man walking fast away from the house.

It would be an understatement to say that Lieutenant Bob Grant was a success. Not only was Bob the supervisor over the Crime Scene section of the Pensacola Police Department, and not only was he revered in his field by all who knew him, but he was the president of the International Association of Crime Scene Analysts. Bob was very detail oriented. He was meticulous almost to a fault. He was the perfect person to lead the crime scene team whose job was to find out what happened. The expert analysts approached the scene methodically and began their investigation. Willie Mae Grayson was lying on the dining room floor, partially covered with a sheet. Kenneth Mitchell had been sitting on the dining room chair when he was attacked. It appeared that both occupants, along with the German Shepherd, were severely hacked to death with the bloody axe found nearby. The house had been ransacked.

Typically, when one person takes the life of another, something changes in the suspect's behavior or routine. He flees or hides, maybe quits a job or school. He yearns to talk to someone, especially someone he knows or trusts. At the very least, his habits change somewhat. Ramon Grayson was no different. He soon found himself wandering the street of his hometown, Federal Way, Washington, looking for friendly faces.

John Hollingsworth figured as much. Almost immediately after Grayson was identified as a suspect, he sent a message to the police in Federal Way with a description of the crime and a request to keep a lookout for Grayson. On April 2, Ramon was spotted at 2 am in a downtown restaurant. He was arrested a short time later walking a few blocks away. He didn't resist and made no statement.

Detective Hollingsworth had a affable and endearing personality. Therefore, So, it was no surprise when Grayson agreed to speak with Hollingsworth. In a recorded statement, he said that a man with a black mask knocked on his grandmother's door and told him that he would "blow my brains out if I didn't get and axe and kill Willie Mae, Kenneth and Freeway." He said he then drank some of the blood.

Soon afterward, Ramon accompanied Detective Hollingsworth and State Attorney Mike Patterson back to Pensacola. They arrived at the airport at 7:30 AM on Saturday, April 7, 1984. Ten days later, the grand jury returned indictments for first-degree murder.

Six months later October 18, Judge Lacey Collier read over the doctor's reports presented to him by Grayson's attorney Dee Loveless. Ten minutes later, Judge Collier ruled that Ramon should be committed to the state mental hospital for treatment. He was unable to understand the severity of the act and could not assist Loveless with a defense. It seemed that justice would never come for Willie Mae and Kenneth, and for Freeway.

Exactly one year after his indictments were returned, Grayson was deemed competent by Judge Collier to assist with his own defense. Due to the horrendous photos and testimony, Grayson opted for a judge trial. It was not a long trial — judge trials are usually quick and have less dramatic effect than jury trials. Usually, presentation of facts and evidence takes most of the time. The trial began on the afternoon of August 12 and was over the next day. Judge Collier wasted no time in coming to a guilty verdict. He then sentenced Grayson to 45 years in prison. The three victims could now rest easier.

The Most Cowardly Act

Two young handsome bachelor police officer roommates. Eric Miller and Jerry Henderson had a great future ahead of them. They could have been brothers. Both had great potential, and both were liked by everyone — almost everyone. Eric was a two-year veteran with the Pensacola Police Department. Jerry was hired as a cadet in January 1983. In 1984, he graduated from the police academy and was promoted to officer on July 31. Finally, he had attained the position that he had always wanted., and he enjoyed the job.

Frank Pericola was a 25-year-old man who frequented his friend's home directly under the officers' apartment at Maison de Ville Apartments. At 4:15 a.m. on November 16, 1984, Pericola, in a drunken stupor, began banging on Miller and Henderson's apartment door. Before either officer could answer Pericola tried forcing the door open. Miller opened the door and confronted Pericola. In a slurred voice and with a beer in his hand, he threatened "I know y'all are cops. I will take care of you."

FRANK E. PERICOLA   JERRY HENDERSON

Miller noticed that Pericola had a Browning 9-millimeter pistol in his pocket and quickly grabbed it. The officers, not wanting to make trouble, simply told Pericola to leave. To their surprise, Pericola pushed Eric and took a fighting stance. The fight was on. After Pericola broke the coffee table and glassware, the officers got him under control. He was charged with Armed Trespass, Carrying a Concealed Firearm, Disorderly Intoxication, and Violently Resisting an Officer.

A month later, on December 14, Jerry arrived at his apartment complex just after midnight. He did not see Frank Pericola cowering in the shadows holding an Uzi automatic rifle, aimed at him. Suddenly, shots rang out and Jerry felt burning sensations in his back, right forearm, and left thigh. Even though in a lot of pain, Jerry managed to see where the shots were coming from and recognize Pericola as the shooter. Amazingly, he calmly got on his police radio and called in the shooting along with the name and description of the suspect, Frank Pericola.

Officer Eric Miller was working at the time and was not at the complex, but Officer John Tucker was. John also lived at the complex and he heard the shots. He heard a car racing away and then saw Jerry lying in a pool of blood. John called for an ambulance and took control of the scene. Other officers hurried to respond, after realizing that one of their own had been shot.

Officer Marsha Smith was one of those that had a sixth sense about finding people. She had often relied on her talent before, but this time was crucial. She immediately felt that Pericola might head for the airport. A short while later, she and Officer Chuck Johnson found Pericola's Jeep there. Johnson also found the rifle. However, Pericola was nowhere in sight.

Police officers often share a sense of kinship with one another. Therefore, when a suspect attacks one of their own, the offense becomes personal. You hurt one of their family, they all feel the pain, and they will not give up until the offender is caught. A manhunt for Pericola followed the shooting. Dennis Norred, chief deputy of the Santa Rosa County Sheriff's Department, got a tip that Pericola was holed up in a trailer in his county. Seven hours after Pericola performed his cowardly stunt, off-duty deputies, the Santa Rosa Sheriff's SWAT team and officers from the Pensacola Police Department surrounded the trailer. On the PA system, Norred ordered the occupant to exit, which he did peacefully. They immediately took him in custody.

Throughout the ordeal, Jerry never lost consciousness. It wasn't known at the time, but one of the bullets struck Jerry's spine. However, he was in great physical shape, and recovered quickly. On January 25, 1985, the Pensacola Police Department held its annual awards banquet. When 22-year-old Jerry Henderson, who was confined to a wheelchair, rolled up to receive the department's Bronze Cross and Blue Star awards, he received a standing ovation.

Leo Thomas was the premier criminal defense attorney in Pensacola. High-priced and highly acclaimed. Pericola's family had hired Leo to represent him, and Leo earned his pay. He had his client committed to the state mental hospital for evaluation, as well as submitted motions and requested hearings, but to no avail. On Monday, November 4, 1985, the day finally arrived that Frank Pericola would answer for his cowardly act to commit attempted murder on one of Pensacola's finest.

The defense maintained that Pericola's five car accidents left him overmedicated and, as a result, he should be absolved of his crime. The jury didn't buy it and, on November 9, Pericola was found guilty. After more competency hearings, Judge Lacey Collier sentenced Pericola on December 23 to life in prison. He was never released. He died in prison in 2017.

Although Jerry Henderson recovered mentally, he never gained the strength back in his legs like he had before. However, that did not keep him from fulfilling his dream of returning to the police department. On September 8, 1986, he was hired as Public Relations Officer of the Pensacola Police Department. Later, he was promoted to Lieutenant of the Public Relations section. After several years, Jerry purchased and ran an automotive specialist business. He later worked in public relations at the Escambia and Santa Rosa County Sheriff's Departments. However, recurring pain caused him to leave law enforcement for good. As of this writing, Jerry stays in touch with police officers in Northwest Florida — a type of hometown hero. Although he stopped chasing bad guys, Jerry Henderson remains the same relentless hometown man whom many people admire and respect. To this day, no one has been able to keep him down — not even a shooting suspect.

HOMES OF THE PENSACOLA POLICE DEPARTMENT

First: Outside the Fort of Pensacola

The first recording of a jail or station house in Pensacola was in 1767. The description of the structure indicates that it might have been no more than a hut, built from the local soft wood. Receipts show that a man named William Arid built the jail on the northeast part of the fort grounds on a tract of land set aside for public and military use. Harcourt and Charlotte: The British have always been known for their orderliness. When they took control of Pensacola, the priority was to design and create a proper town. This meant laying out streets that were equal in size and distance apart. Lots were drawn up and laid out equally. The existing streets were renamed for British politicians, statesmen and heroes and new ones were given British names. A British surveyor, Elias Durnford, was commissioned to do the layout. The jail was assigned to the northeast corner of the fort compound on the outside of the fort itself. The site was located on the Southwest corner of Alcaniz and Intendencia Streets. It began as a small wooden building. No pictures of the small lockup exist.

Second: Intendencia and Alcaniz Streets

In 1776, Joseph Purcell drew up a new map. Included in the map was a building labeled "Prison, a brick building" within the garrison (Granby and Charlotte Streets). In 1778, as the city expanded, another Pensacola map of Joseph Purcell showed a "*Gaol* (old Spanish word for jail), built of brick." The small building was located on the Southwest corner of Alcaniz and Intendencia Streets, the same location — just different street names.

Economic expansion became one of the byproducts of the new waterfront town. Of course, this was a two-edged sword. The money that sailors are paid must be spent. The crime rates increased, making it necessary to build a new jail. Pensacolians referred to the creepy ramshackle old structure of a jail as the "Old Calaboose." In the late 1700s, the calaboose was built on the southwest corner of Alcaniz and Intendencia Streets. In 1822, Governor George Walton wrote in the territorial papers that all the buildings in the town were wooden and old "except the jail, which is a miserable building." In 1835, the calaboose was in such a state of disrepair that the city finally decided to tear it down.

Third: Zarragossa & Adams Streets

On August 2, 1824, the Pensacola Gazette published an article stating that the town of Pensacola had repaired the basement of the old Government House and turned it into a jail. The station was temporary — until the old calaboose was razed and another built. The building was located on Zarragossa Street approximately 100 feet west of Adams Street on the north side of the road.

Fourth: Tarragona & Government Streets

John Lee Williams was a lawyer in Pensacola. He was apparently also a mapmaker. In 1827, he completed a map of downtown Pensacola. One of the buildings is labeled "Court Ho and Jail." The building is located on the northeast corner of today's Tarragona & Government Streets.

Fifth: Alcaniz & Intendencia Streets

On April 12, 1838, The *Pensacola Gazette* contained the following article:

> *In 1836 the city erected a good and substantial jail on the site of the old Spanish Calaboose. This building was a two-story brick building. The bottom floor was for the prisoners, and the cell which housed all of them was 15 feet by 16 feet. The second floor was where Fransisco Touart and his family lived. Touart's*

duties included looking after the peace and quiet of the city, committing and releasing prisoners, ringing the city bell on all proper occasions, and feeding the prisoners.

Sixth: Palafox & Main Streets

The Civil War brought, among other changes, the buying and selling of many properties. Two years after Lee surrendered, the Pfieffer brothers — Henry and George, owned the "Old Market House" at the corner of Palafox and Main Streets. From 1867 to 1882, they allowed the city to rent a room there for use as a jail.

Seventh: Tarragona & Main Streets

With a larger department came the need for a larger headquarters. This problem presented itself almost immediately upon reorganizing. Finally, in 1887, the department moved to a building located on the northwest corner of Tarragona and Main Streets.

Eighth: Jefferson and Zarragossa Streets

A result of the new provisional municipality was a decision that was made to erect a new building to house the city hall and jail. The new building was to be built on the southwest corner of Jefferson and Zarragossa Streets. In 1889, the announcement was made. The city now had a new building in which it could conduct business. The modern facility held a police office, jail cells, and an apartment on the first floor. The marshal's office and the police court were located on the second floor. The city commissioners held regular meetings in the courtroom upstairs.

Ninth: Jefferson and Zarragossa Streets

After sixteen years together, the agreement was made to separate city hall business and police business. A new city hall was built directly east of Plaza Ferdinand. To provide for construction of the new police headquarters, the police department, in 1906, temporarily occupied the building on the southwest corner of Jefferson and Zarragossa streets.

Tenth: 407 S. Jefferson Street

On February 29, 1908, the new police station, located on the Northwest corner of Jefferson and Main, was ready. At a cost of $4,011.67, it was turned over to the police officials at 11 AM. They immediately began

Chief Sanders and members of the Pensacola Police Department in front of the police station

moving furniture in. It had a front desk and lobby, two telephones, offices for policemen, a modern jail, a kitchen, and office facilities for the marshal and chief. A ten-foot wall was erected around the entire building so children could not see prisoners.

Eleventh: 40 South Alcaniz Street

Under Chief Hall's direction, many changes occurred. On August 5, 1956, the new police headquarters and jail were opened for business. The location was 40 south Alcaniz Street on the south side of St. Michael's Cemetery. The two-story building was described by the local news as a modern crime-fighting structure, complete with a detective bureau, a records section, and an entire jail facility which included a kitchen for cooking meals for the inmates. The north end of the building was occupied by the U. S. Navy Shore Patrol.

Some prisoners named them. The rats in the city jail were so regular that they became friends to the bored inmates. By 1980, the city jail that took up a lot of space in the police department was old, smelly, vermin-ridden, and hot. The lighting, which existed only in the hallway, was dim. Instead of prisoners being issued jail jumpsuits daily, they simply wore their underwear due to the often 100+ degree temperature. In June 1980, local attorney Ron Shelley filed a class-action lawsuit in federal court claiming poor jail conditions and police brutality. Shelley had filed a similar lawsuit against the county jail a few months earlier. The city jail only housed pretrial detainees, and there were usually only about 20 city prisoners at any given time. Deplorable conditions, fights, a federal lawsuit, and ever-increasing mandates helped the city fathers decide which route to take. They offered to pay Escambia County $38 per inmate per day to house them. The county commissioners agreed to build a new multimillion-dollar jail as a response to the lawsuit. As a result, the city jail closed in early 1982, leaving the old

Pensacola Police Department's 13th home — 40 S. Alcaniz Street

building on Alcaniz Street as a police administrative office building only. The jail burden felt like a weight lifted. One dark spot was losing "Miss Lucy." Lucy Jordan, the city jail cook, was forced to resign after 17 years. Miss Lucy's cooking was so good that some inmates looked forward to being locked up so they could eat her cooking. Officers also felt like that since Miss Lucy cooked for them as well. An era had come to an end.

Twelfth: 711 N. Hayne Street

The Alcaniz Street station was an old building. The roof leaked; the old carpet smelled. Most of the old jail was no longer used. Since the U.S. Navy's Shore Patrol had vacated the north part of the building, it was not used either. The parking lot offered little room for vehicles, and the location was in a flood plain. In addition, the new demands for the department, and for the law enforcement profession called for a new building design (more room needed for Communication section, Investigations, etc.) It was time for a new station at a new location. The site chosen was one that was immediately available — under Interstate 110 between Jackson Street

Pensacola Police Headquarters, 711 N. Hayne Street

and Cervantes Street. An architect was hired, inquiries were made, and several key officers were consulted to come up with the best design so the construction could begin. The seven years from the filing of the lawsuit to the opening of the new building saw both buildings abuzz with activity! Finally, in October 1987, officers and movers worked quickly relocating to the new building at 711 North Hayne Street. The new, modern building offered roomier offices, a state-of-the-art Communications section, a quality training section, and a first-rate Patrol section.

On February 5, 2019, the author interviewed one of the officers who was crucial in bringing about the building of the police station on Hayne Street. Lt. Charlie DeCosta was born on December 16, 1941 in Jacksonville. In 1959, Charlie found himself stationed onboard an aircraft carrier in Pensacola. In 1963, he returned to Pensacola and began looking for a career-worthy job. He received offers to interview with the postal service and with the police department. He chose to become a police officer and began his 31-year career on August 5, 1967. In the early 1980s, the need for a new police headquarters arose. It was determined that the cost to build a new building would be less than remodeling the old one. Chief Goss chose Charlie to share his ideas and opinions about the new building's design. Finally, the department relocated to the new, 31,000 square foot building. The two-million-dollar building was designed by Donald Lindsey and built by the Norton — DelGallo Company. It was truly a practical building to be proud of, with a lot of thought put into the location of offices and adjacent meeting rooms, communication centers, etc.

As a part of Chief Lou Goss' retirement ceremony on December 31, 1994, the building was officially named "The Louis Goss Police Headquarters."

SPOTLIGHTS

The Godfather

The scene could be at any business, home, or situation: Chaos everywhere, emotions running high, things said that would later be regretted, insurmountable problems. Then he walks in. Quiet and calm, he stops, looks around, and says a few words. It's over. No more problems. Order has been restored. The Godfather has spoken.

That was Raymond Harper. Known as the Godfather of the Pensacola Police Department, Captain Harper was a cornerstone of law enforcement in West Florida. He didn't rule from a position of fear; he ruled from respect and love. He knew how to diffuse a chaotic situation by saying a few simple words. Anyone who knew Raymond remember him as a peaceful, slightly overweight man who often had a pipe in his mouth.

Captain Raymond Harper

Raymond was born in 1918 in Pensacola. His dad was PPD Chief E. E. Harper of the 1920s. Eventually, Chief Harper became the police commissioner. Thus, Raymond had excellent training. He grew up in law enforcement, probably hanging around the department as a child. He always knew he wanted to be a Pensacola Police officer.

As a teenager, Raymond got to know Escambia County Sheriff Hamp Gandy. As soon as Raymond turned 18, Gandy employed him with the title of "Special Deputy." A year later, he joined the Pensacola Police Department. The January 2, 1941 edition of the Pensacola News Journal stated that

Raymond, Ed Lawhorn, and Billy Kelson would be hired "for a six-month trial period." Chief Willie O'Connor gave him his first beat assignment — in the heart of downtown. Downtown? In the days before WWII, downtown Pensacola was rough. Bars, gambling houses, the red-light district, dance halls — all the action happened there. The clientele were the rough and tumble men from the pine forests in the northern part of the county and the sailors from the U. S. Navy and from private ships from across the globe. Whenever one of the ruffians had too many spirits inside and didn't like the idea of going to jail, the fight was on. No backup, no radio, it was either whip your arrestee or he whipped you. That was the "rookie school" that Raymond Harper attended.

Was Raymond rough? Yes. Was Raymond mean? No. He wasn't a fighter, although he had to fight often. He was a peaceable man. So, he quickly learned that his best quality was his ability to talk things out. He often convinced drunks to come to jail quietly or talked down an escalating situation. He once recalled that he was summoned to a home on a disturbance call. When he arrived and knocked on the door, a man answered for Raymond to enter. When he got inside, he took in the situation. The man was holding two pistols on two Pensacola Police officers who were in a corner with their hands up. Tension filled the air, but Raymond recognized the man as an old high school buddy. As he began talking to the man, he inched closer. "You don't want to shoot your ole buddy, do you?" He slowed approached the man until he was standing in front of his pistol. He said "Now, just give me the gun." The man replied, "You're right, Raymond. Seeing how it's you, I'll give the gun to you."

Raymond worked his way from patrolman to investigator to sergeant to motorcycle officer to captain. His career suited him so well that it seemed as though he had always been Captain Harper. He was more concerned for everyone else than he was himself. He had either trained or supervised everyone who captain or chief. He wasn't only the rock that held the department together — he was a friend and mentor. When someone was around Raymond, they felt a connection with him. He was a friend to everybody, even children.

Raymond held two things close to his heart: the Pensacola Police Department and his family. He and his wife, Melba, lived in the 2000 block of West Romana for years until they moved to 12th Avenue and High Pine Place. Raymond began his PPD career on January 15, 1941 and retired on January 15, 1981 — 40 years of being a law enforcement anchor. He died on Monday evening, December 14, 1987, at age 68.

A Real Street Cop

Everyone that has seen a television cop show has seen him. The streetwise cop. He chases down the bad guy, throws him against the fence, and twists his arm so badly that he gives up the information that the cop wants. Or he threatens the guy with his life if he doesn't get the info, and the guy always complies out of fear. Does that happen? Yes. Often? No.

That is the fallacy that exists in the minds of citizens and new officers. Why? Because they see it on TV, so it must be right. Right? Wrong. A real street cop is the straight shooter that knows what is happening on his beat, where to get the information he needs and already has established a relationship with the people on the street.

Being a real street cop takes work. Consequently, few cops are street cops. Why? Because it's more advantageous for an officer to spend his or her energy and focus on moving up the career ladder. A street cop is motivated by being important to those on his beat. If you ever want to know which officers are important to citizens, ask them. A street cop has a relationship with them.

Few officers are renowned by the people in their area. People don't recognize a real street cop by seeing his picture in the paper or his face on television. They *KNOW* him. Occasionally, an officer will come along who is not only known, but missed when he is not seen, or after he retires. But, like a good mailman, when a police officer is gone, he is not missed over about 30 days…except for officers like Henry Cassady. For 10 years after he retired, people would ask about him — fondly.

As the old saying goes, "When a cop is 19, he chases 19-year-olds. When he is 29, he is still chasing 19-year-olds, when he is 39, he is still chasing 19-year-olds. When he is 49, he is still chasing 19-year-olds. When Henry was young, he chased — and caught — suspects. As he got older and wiser, he discovered the best way was if the people knew and trusted him. If a young person had a warrant, Henry probably knew him or his parents or grandparents. They knew him and trusted him. He got what was needed.

"Cassdy." That is how he is known to many. Any member of the Pensacola Police Department who has worked on the street in the 1970s — 2000s has been asked "Is Cassdy workin'?" or "Do you know Cassdy?" If you answered in the affirmative, you were hailed as a friend, because you, like them, knew Cassdy. Henry Cassady knew people. He was as comfortable eating with the regulars at the old Grand Hotel in one of the roughest areas of town as he was with the richest lawyer or politician — and they all knew him. They all knew him *personally*. And he treated them with respect. Even as he arrested people, he respected them. That reputation grew. People knew that "Cassdy" wouldn't

Sergeant Henry Cassady

do them wrong. He treated people right, so he was treated right. More than once, citizens stood up for Cassady in defiance of someone bent on causing harm. If Cassady needed information, he got it, because people trusted that he needed it for the right reason, and he wouldn't abuse that trust.

Don't misunderstand — if a person needed to go to jail, Henry took them to jail. If they needed to be talked to, Henry talked — and listened. Henry did what needed to be done. But citizens knew that he only took the action that was necessary. He treated people right. Henry was liked and respected by citizens of all classes in Pensacola.

The relationships he had with citizens though, paled in comparison to the relationships he had with the other members of the police department. He would treat everyone — from the chief to the newest cadet — the same. If an officer needed reprimanding, he reprimanded. If they needed praising, he praised. One instance occurred in the late 1980s. It was a busy weekday morning, and Chief Louis Goss called on the radio,

"Unit 1 to Headquarters" said the boss.

"Go ahead, Unit 1."

"There is a drunk (man) lying beside the road on Palafox Street. Send somebody to get him up." No answer…everyone was tied up. Then, more authoritatively, the big chief with the booming voice said,

"Did you hear me? Somebody needs to take care of this drunk!" Still no answer…long pause…Finally, Sgt. Cassady came on the radio.

"Chief, we ain't got nobody. We're all busy. Handle him yourself." Everyone was convinced that Henry Cassady was history. He was going to be fired.

"Uh…10-4" came the humbled answer. Nothing else was said.

Henry Cassady believed in his officers, and he made them believe in themselves. He didn't sugar coat the world, but he taught his officers how to work through it. And he taught his officers how to treat people right. He also trusted his officers, and they trusted him. One night, a silent alarm sounded at the police communications center, and the radio sounded with the traditional beeps. The dispatcher came on the air,

"0-23 (armed robbery) at the Circle K at 12th Avenue and Cervantes." Five seconds later, two plain clothes officers in an unmarked car arrived.

"We are in pursuit of a dark-colored sedan with his headlights off, heading north on 12th Avenue." A few seconds went by.

"Headquarters, they are shooting at us!" A few more seconds.

"Looks like they are bailing out at 12th and Anderson. Send two K9s." …A few more seconds…

"Shots fired! Keep one K9 coming but now send one ambulance." …A few more seconds…

"Shots fired again! Cancel the K9s but send two ambulances!" As units raced to the aid of the two officers involved, Sgt. Cassady arrived first. The officers did not work for Henry. He said "Okay, tell me what happened." When he heard what happened, he said "You did right. Don't talk to anyone else. Tell them to contact me." He took care of everything. He became the young officers' spokesman.

Henry grew up in Santa Rosa county, that county that he still lives in as of this writing. After high school, he went into the U. S. Army as a paratrooper. After his discharge, he joined the Pensacola Police Department in 1967. He worked as a patrolman, detective, in Vice, and as a sergeant, where he worked in Tac, Investigations, and Patrol. He and his wife Julia have three children.

Henry Cassady's reputation was this — if he told you something, it was the truth — good or bad. Henry is the real deal. That is a cop.

The Trailblazer

Dixie Jo — sounds like a name in a movie. That is a southern name. And Dixie is the epitome of a southern girl — a great deal of sweetness and strength. That describes her. She was born and raised in Pensacola, something that is important to her. As a matter of fact, one could argue that Dixie IS Pensacola. Her family has been an integral part of the city for many years. Her grandfather, Charles Millard Kelson was a Police officer in the early 1920s. Her uncle, William "Billy" Kelson, was also an officer in the 1940s and 50s. Both also served as Constables during their law enforcement days. Her father, Kenneth, served as a City Commissioner *and* a County Commissioner, which is rare.

Dixie Chancellor

Kenneth Kelson had a lot of common sense, and he used it well to guide the city and the county through rough waters during the 20th Century. His daughter takes after him.

As a child, Dixie wanted to train horses and own a horse ranch. When she grew up, she fulfilled her desire; she moved to the countryside and bought several horses. Her love for Pensacola and for the Pensacola Police Department has always been a part of her, just as her family has — her son Cole and husband Mike Wilkinson, a retired Pensacola Police Sergeant. She began working at the department when she was a teenager. In a time when most women were glad that they could get a job, she quietly blazed a trail into a male-dominated world. She started in Records, but soon transferred to the traditionally male-dominated Crime Scene, which she loved. However, she said that it was not a good feeling when she had to stand next to serial killer Ted Bundy and process his prints.

Eventually, she supervised the Records division, also normally a "men-only" position. She later transferred to the Communications Section to become a dispatcher. As a dispatcher, Dixie felt what all dispatchers feel. While doing everything in their power to help their police officers, they feel an overwhelming frustration when tragedy strikes, and they can't help or be there. One of Dixie's low moments occurred when she lost an officer — something that happened three times to her. She also disliked the long, tired, frustrating hours of working through Hurricane Ivan in 2004. However, she and the other dispatchers who she supervised, continued onward and were able to assist their officers during troubling times. When Dixie began working as a dispatcher, female employment in her line of work was still in its infancy. Nevertheless, Dixie not only continued at her job, but she also improved working conditions in the Communications arena.

She had found her niche. She was good at it, and she loved it! Soon, she was promoted to supervisor, becoming the first female at the department to wear stripes on her uniform. Eventually, the department appointed her to an unprecedented position — she was placed over both Records and Communications — a lieutenant's position that had never been done before.

Dixie retired on June 16, 2008 after 35 years of blazing new trails.

A Living Legend

To envision something before it exists is a rare talent. Most people can see something and may be able to see the potential of it, but few people can take and idea and look at it in its entirety. Mack Cramer can do that. Mack is a man of vision.

On February 19, 2019, the author interviewed Retired Officer Mack Cramer: Mack was born in 1949 in Charleston, S. C. He grew up in a small town just East of New Orleans called Saint Bernard, LA. He always wanted to be a veterinarian. At age 25, Mack had a family, but no job. And he needed a job — bad. The Comprehensive Employment and Training Act (CETA) provided jobs for people in public service. Not entirely sure what that meant, Mack thought that sounded good, so he applied. They sent him to a town on the northwestern tip of Florida called Pensacola. A police officer wasn't a veterinarian, but it was a job — and Mack needed a job. When he sat down for his employment interview, Mack said, "…Captain Haner was on my oral board and he asked me 'Why do you want to be a police officer?' I replied, 'Sir you are hiring, and I need a job.' I came out third on the list." A family man, Mack and his wife, Sandra, have five children: Johnathan, Chrissy, Mark, Terry, and Pam — he needed a job! He began in 1974.

According to the website: http://www.fayar.net/sro/sroprogram.html, in the late 1950's, the first School Resource Officer program was started in Flint, Michigan. Its overall goal was to improve the relationship between the local police and youth. Officers were placed in schools on a full-time basis to serve as teachers and counselors. The program became a huge success and Flint, Michigan and became a model for school resource officer programs across the country.

For 10 years, Mack worked on the streets. As a police officer, it is sometimes frustrating to see a young life destroyed by drugs and crime — especially if someone could have gotten to them earlier and made a difference in their lives. Yet, it would require total dedication from a person to make that difference. Both police officers and teachers could do this. However, if it were possible to be a police officer and a teacher, the impact would be even greater. Even if police officers were assigned to a school, that would be valuable. What a vision!

Mack said "I first heard of the program in 1984. I began researching it and presented it to Lt. Jim Billy Barnes. He liked it, so we went to Chief Goss about the idea. After reviewing the program, his response was 'Do it. Make it work' and of course the rest is history."

In the 1984–85 school year, Pensacola High School introduced a new aspect — *School Resource Officer Mack Cramer*. No one knew if the program would work. It was a trial. The Pensacola Police Department and the Escambia County School District had gone in on a 50/50 deal, and neither were certain it was worth the investment. A police officer must have tough skin and be able to withstand name-calling and hatred that he or she receives on the job. Students, parents, teachers, administrators all had opinions and comments about a police officer working at a school. But the success of the program was left with Mack Cramer, and how he responded.

Pensacola High School

Mack described the feeling, "The day I went to PHS was the beginning of a program that has truly impacted the Pensacola Police Department, the School system and the lives of literally thousands of kids. I can't tell you how many kids that now see me in the community that walk up to me and say "You're Officer Cramer, aren't you?" and of course I reply "Yes I am." Most shake my hand, hug me and tell me what an impact I had on them."

There is a saying "Everyone has the same 24 hours in a day. It's not the hours, it's how you use them." Well, people might not believe that Mack Cramer had only 24 hours in a day. In addition to being a School Resource Officer, he coached the Junior Varsity football team and the Junior Varsity Baseball team. He taught a criminal Justice class every day. He taught Drivers Education and Drug Prevention each semester. He visited many classrooms, teaching mainly on the 4th amendment, and he held the Police Explorer Program classes in the school every Tuesday. He sponsored the SADD (students against driving drunk) program at PHS. He also taught a class for teachers on how to report criminal activity, as well as a courtroom demeanor class in case teachers needed to testify in court. An enjoyable class he taught was how to act when stopped on the streets by Police Officers to those with learning disabilities. In short, Mack did whatever was necessary to make a difference.

The SRO program was such a huge success that the other high school in the city limits — Booker T. Washington, began the same program. This was followed by Workman Middle School. The SRO program also led the way for the DARE program to be started in the elementary schools. Escambia County and the other counties in West Florida followed suit and developed SRO programs in their schools. However, the dean of the SROs in all the Florida panhandle was Mack Cramer. Mack found other opportunities because of his position. He taught classes, helped coach teams, and started a successful Police Explorer program at the school. He also advanced through the NASRO (National Association of School Resource Officers) program to become a School Resource Officer Practitioner, the highest qualification an officer can receive in the SRO program.

Today's SRO program is a vital part of most law enforcement agencies. A school resource officer conducts daily law enforcement duties, but also often acts as a counselor, advisor, teacher, and role model for students and teachers. Most schools cannot imagine not having an SRO in their institution.

Mack Cramer retired from the Pensacola Police Department in 2000, after having created one of the most successful programs in the history of the department. Ironically, the highlight of his association with the police department came after his retirement. He pinned a PPD badge on the chest of his son, Johnathan (who eventually became a school resource officer). As a man of vision, Mack Cramer successfully turned a simple idea into the SRO program that we know today. He also educated and aided many children and staff members, and he was a great role model for the students who needed direction. Whether or not he envisioned it would become an integral part of the department is not known. However, in the eyes of thousands of men and women in Pensacola and elsewhere, Mack Cramer is a living legend.

The Ultimate Boss

While working at the Pensacola Police Department, the author often instructed police classes. The number one answer to the question "Who is the best example of a supervisor?" was *ALWAYS* "Mike Thompson."

Sergeant Mike Thompson

Mike Thompson, a longtime sergeant at the Pensacola Police Department, would bring out the best in his officers, and the officers who worked around him. Mike was a pleasure to be around. Anywhere Mike was, other officers usually gathered around. Most didn't know it, but the reason was that Mike made them feel good about themselves. They wanted to do a good job for Mike, so they worked harder.

When a young officer who just chased and caught a suspect was approached by two sergeants — his own supervisor and Mike Thompson. While the rookie's sergeant didn't say anything, Mike congratulated the officer on a job well done. It made the rookie's day.

Most officers who were promoted to supervisor in the Pensacola Police Department tried "to be like Mike." He was probably one of the most unselfish members in the department's history. As he neared retirement, being a senior supervisor, he could have the new vehicles if he desired — especially since he drove an old unmarked car that had been in a crash and never repaired. However, he decided to let a younger officer drive the new car, and he kept driving the old wreck of a car.

However, don't ever mistake of confusing Mike for being a softy. As often as Mike would smile and encourage his officers, he would also hold suspects accountable.

Mike's skills flowed through his family too, as his son Shawnn joined the force when Mike retired. Shawn quickly proved himself to be a great officer, sergeant, and lieutenant, following in the footsteps of his father. After all, he had a good teacher.

He's Got Your Back

"A man ought to do what he thinks is best."
—John Wayne

Captain George Underwood

Anyone who knows Captain George Underwood knows these things about him: He is a patriot, he is a Marine, and he is a John Wayne fan. Once a person got to know him, he or she quickly found out something else about him — he had your back. For many years, George was the captain of the Uniform Patrol Division — the largest division of the police department. This is probably the most stressful position in the entire department. It is large, has all the rookies, and deals with the vast majority of the first responses. Typically, if an officer finds himself called to the captain's office, his day probably just took a turn for the worse. So, an officer generally views the captain of that division as he would a bear — stay away, and whatever you do, don't antagonize him.

George Underwood was different. Don't get me wrong — if you did wrong, the bear came out in him, and all I can say is…God bless you. But, if you did what you thought was right, George always tried to understand. Mistakes happen. Accidents happen. And, whatever the case, Captain Underwood had your back. On many occasions, officers were defended by George as vigorously as a defense attorney defends his client.

It seemed that George Underwood has always believed in the good in people. It was probably not the case, but he seemed to like everyone. One thing about George: You knew — no matter what happened — you were going to get a fair shake with George.

FIRSTS

The First Minority Police Officer

A police officer in 1882 did not require much education, and the pay was not great. However, the position has always carried with it a certain amount of prestige and authority over others. Although the War Between the States was over, many state and local governments were not willing to put persons of color in charge of others. Many cities had no black police officers until the 1950s or 1960s. There were exceptions, of course. One of the most feared and respected law officers was Deputy Marshal Bass Reeves, 1838–1910. In addition, Daniel Hale Williams was a famous physician, and John Sweat Rock was a successful attorney. But…a police officer? Authority over other people? A black man? However, as has been noted previously, Pensacola was not a typical southern town. Racial problems in Pensacola were not as significant as it was in many towns — north or south.

An African-American Police Officer during reconstruction

This is not to say that Pensacola was without racial pressures and problems. Following the War Between the States, southern sympathizers established "Black Codes" that kept newly freed African Americans, called "Freedmen," from becoming truly free. In 1865, Congress enacted the Bureau of Refugees, Freedmen and Abandoned Lands, known as the Freedmen's Bureau, to assist blacks and destitute whites financially. The Bureau ushered in an unprecedented move on the part of the city fathers. Two

African American men were hired as Pensacola Police Officers. Though their names are not known, integration was established in Pensacola.

The presence of the Freedmen's Bureau and the military kept racial tensions down but did not eliminate them entirely. According to Ralph Peek in his book *Lawlessness and the Restoration of Order in Florida: 1868–1871*, in September 1868, an unknown black Pensacola police officer was shot three times and would have been killed had another person not stopped him. However, many of the white people in the town were not concerned for the officer's well-being. A few days later, another unknown black Pensacola police officer, seeing trouble brewing, refused to arrest a white lawbreaker. He carried through with the arrest only after his white supervisor ordered him to do so.

The first identified Pensacola Police Officer of color is mentioned in a column in the August 1, 1882 edition of the *Pensacola Commercial*. It reads "Policeman Cook (colored), well and favorably known hereabouts has been restored to his position on the police force of the city, much to the delectation of his numerous friends, who may be counted by scores in all races as well as shades of political bias. He will be in charge of the Street Brigade, and under his direction it is said more, and better work can be accomplished than under any member of the force. It is hoped that he will give any genius he may have in this direction 'full play,' as our thoroughfares are certainly much in need of it." Three days later, the following appeared in *The Pensacola Commercial* newspaper: "On yesterday morning, Thos. Glennon was fined $10 in the police court for shooting at police officer Smith Campbell, colored. Mr. Glennon was afterwards arrested on a peace warrant sworn out by Campbell and taken before Judge Shackelford, who required him to enter into a bond with security to observe the peace towards Campbell for twelve months."

First Police Motorcycle

1912: Mike Murphy was a 38-year-old officer with the PPD. Mike, who began his career in 1903, was from Ireland. He was a tough man and was in great shape. Any time someone ran from him, fleet-footed Mike simply outran him…until those motorized vehicles arrived. Mike Murphy was frustrated. "Why can't we get one of those motorcycles?" he asked his captain. "You know, they have been around for more than 10 years. More people are getting them, along with those auto-mobiles. We need to keep up."

The captain thought about it. The next day, he approached Marshal Sanders, who liked the idea. "Maybe I can get one for me!" Mike said. The marshal took the idea to the next city commission meeting and pitched the idea. To his surprise, the entire commission was in favor.

In 1913, the department acquired its first motorcycle. The January 4, 1913 edition of the *Pensacola News Journal* read "the chief of police notified the board that the motorcycle for use in the police department will arrive in the city in fourteen days. It is a 1913 model machine and will be the first one ever used in the police department of this city." The January 16 edition informed that the machine had arrived. Although the maker of it was not listed, it was said that the motorcycle could travel 90 miles an hour, and it had a speedometer! The cost was $250.

On May 24, 1944, the *Pensacola News Journal* ran an article. The Pensacola Police motorcycle officers were sporting their summer khaki uniforms and their brand new 1944 Harley-Davidson motorcycles. They had just added three new ones to the ones they already had. In 1950, the city officials decided to outfit each motorcycle with one of the new two-way radios. The cost

Pensacola Police Motorcycle Unit

was $622.30 each, or $530 each if they were installed on new motorcycles at the factory. On February 27, 1970, the city accepted an officer for three new motorcycles from Hero Motorcycle for a total of $6276.57.

When motorcycles first arrived on the market, they were purchased out of necessity. Motorcycles are very practical in heavy traffic or crowds. As time went on, the romantic aspect of a cop on a motorcycle became more evident. Eventually, police motorcycles became a way for Pensacola to "show off." Anytime flashy or shiny is needed, the motorcycles are used. Hero, Kawasaki, Harley — whatever the Pensacola Police Motor Officers drive, they do it in style — especially if they make it more than a few months before crashing!

First Police Automobile

In the early 1900s, gasoline powered vehicles were abundant in Pensacola. However, the Pensacola Police Department only owned horses and one wagon, which was used by the chief or the captain. Most of the officers walked a beat. Finally, the department bought a motorcycle.

With Henry Ford's mass production of the automobile, officers soon realized the value of cars used for police work. An officer in a police car could cover more area than several officers on foot. Also, the need for police cars was growing because the Pensacola police had no way to catch the drivers of the new automobiles. With the increase in the number of cars in the city, the sand and clay streets of Pensacola were slowly being replaced

The First Pensacola Police Car, Chief Sanders Driving, Mayor Greenhut, Left Rear

with creosote wooden blocks that were as hard as bricks. More automobiles and better roads paved the way for police motor vehicles.

In November 1913, discussion and approval took place at the regular meeting of the city commissioners regarding allowing for $600 for an automobile for Chief Sanders. On November 29, the *Pensacola News Journal* reported that the police department had purchased a large, four-door used Ford for $950 to be used primarily by the chief, but also by the commissioners. Pensacola finally had its first police car!

Pensacola's First Traffic Light

Euclid Avenue and East 105th Street. That is where it went. The city officials decided that the busy intersection is where the world's first traffic light was needed. The year was 1914 and the city was Cleveland, Ohio. Earlier, in 1912, Police Officer Lester Wire developed the first traffic light in Salt Lake City, Utah, but it was not yet installed.

The Opinion page of the *Pensacola News Journal* on February 10, 1924 read, "Another chance to save a few dollars is for the commissioners to forget about that traffic signal system they contemplate putting up at Garden and Palafox streets. This is a useless expenditure of public funds, when the application of a little common sense is all that is needed."

Fortunately for the citizens of Pensacola, Commissioner of Police E. E. Harper, didn't listen to the News Journal. On December 20, 1925, the first traffic light in Pensacola began operating at Palafox and Garden streets, with police officers stationed at the intersection to educate the public regarding their use. There is no report as to the identity of the first person to intentionally run the light.

First Female Pensacola Police Officer

It was a first. It happened on January 7, 1974. Jeri Schadee, Alfred "Skip" Bollens and Gary Stewart were sworn in as Pensacola Police Officers in Chief Caldwell's office. Not that the ceremony was a first, because it wasn't. It is required for an officer to be sworn before taking official action. However, never had a woman been sworn in as a Pensacola Police Officer before. Jeri was not new to the police department. She was already employed there. On Monday, January 31, 2019, the author interviewed Officer Schadee.

Jeri Schadee had been in the military already when, in 1965, she was offered the position of records clerk at age 27. It wasn't that she had always wanted to work in the police environment, but, as she put it…she simply needed a job. From records clerk, a position in the ID section opened and she applied. Not knowing how to take fingerprints or photos, or how to process a crime scene, she didn't feel the probability of her getting the job was likely. However, she did! She learned not only how to take fingerprints, but how to identify suspects by their prints. During her eight years in the station among the officers, she learned the radio signals, police lingo, and, as a records clerk, she was more familiar with the state statutes and city ordinances than many of the officers. Then, in 1972, a position opened for police officer. Never had a female been hired as a Pensacola police officer before, and most officers thought it still wouldn't happen, but Jeri felt it important to apply. She said that they were going to have to turn her down to her face! Besides, she was now 35 years old, which was the maximum age for applying for police officer. So, it was to everyone's surprise when Chief Caldwell contacted Jeri and asked her if she wanted the job!

Swearing-in ceremony, January 7, 1974
L-R: Jeri Schadee, Skip Bollens, Gary Stewart being sworn in by Chief Caldwell

Many of the officers were less than thrilled about a woman entering their ranks, convinced that she wouldn't be able to do the job. Jeri said that many officers talked down to her and outwardly let everyone know that they didn't want her to respond as a backup for their calls. They wanted a male officer to respond. She said that there were even times when she would be sent on a call that required two officers, but no one would back her up. She said that among the crude remarks and propositions, there were a few officers who supported her, but they were not allowed to do so in front of other officers or supervisors.

The public also treated her differently. In general, people preferred to have a male officer respond to their problem. "Interesting," said Jeri "the black men were mostly reticent," preferring to work well with her and show her respect.

Jeri, a petit woman, said that she could not compete with men using the same methods — she wasn't as big or as strong as they were, so she had to approach situations in a manner that no one could teach in any academy. She approached people with tact — like a lady, requesting their cooperation instead of demanding it. Not only did it work, but Jeri proved that females are indispensable in the police profession! Females are more effective in some undercover situations and often establish a better rapport with victims, especially in sexual assault cases. Jeri's approach to policing was taught to new officers well into the 21st century. When asked if she would do it all over again, Jeri beamed "ABSOLUTELY!"

The First African American Captain

He was likeable. He wasn't a large man — sort of skinny. One officer described him as "loving a good joke. He always made people feel good about themselves. However, if need be, he had no problem going to the mat with anyone. Tim Poe wasn't scared!"

Captain Tim Poe

As a patrol officer, Tim would interview, not intimidate a person. He or she usually ended up confessing, but not because Tim forced him or her. A person simply wanted to tell him about it because he or she liked Tim. Tim was a Pensacola native, so he knew a lot of people. Right out of high school, he joined the military, then came back to Pensacola to join the force. He spoke straight about things. For many years, he served as the sergeant in the detective bureau, and made some crucial decisions with some mighty big cases.

Tim Poe was smart — very smart. To speak with him, one felt as though he was very educated, but he made everyone feel comfortable around him. He was well-versed, well-read, and well-spoken. Most people didn't know that Tim possessed a bachelor's degree, but not the advanced degrees that he appeared to have. He was promoted to sergeant in 1976, to lieutenant in 1980, and to captain in 1995. He retired in 1998 and died of cancer in 2006.

The First Female Patrol Sergeant

Officer Tonya Humprhies was more interested in doing the right thing than aggressive policing. She liked to shoot straight with people (pun intended) and give them the benefit of the doubt.

Sergeant Tonya Humphries

She was hired as a police officer in 1986. Just like the men, she worked hard. As a matter of fact, she worked harder. She had to. Police work for a female is an uphill journey. She worked shift work in the worst areas and handled the worst calls, all with a smile. As a detective, she never made more of a case than it was. She took things at face value and did her job. As a female, her chances of promotion were not good. No female police officer had ever been promoted in the history of the Pensacola Police Department. So, when she had proven herself, she decided to take the sergeant's exam in 1999 in hopes of promotion — against all odds.

She was promoted on Thursday, December 23, 1999. Did she have any trouble from officers who refused to take orders from a woman? The author interviewed Sgt. Humphries on August 5, 2019 and asked her that question. She related several instances in which male officers refused to follow her orders, and on two occasions downright defied them. After written reprimands, officers soon acknowledged her for her authority. The same toughness that got her the position kept her there.

The First Female Captain

Kristin Brown joined the Pensacola Police Department in 1996 as a cadet. From cadet to officer to sergeant and, on July 31, 2015, she was the first female promoted to patrol lieutenant. On May 23, 2017, she was pinned as the first female captain of the department.

On August 6, 2019, the author interviewed Captain Brown. When asked what the secret to her success was, Kristin replied that she gives credit to her parents. She said that they worked hard to instill in her a hard work ethic and a habit of discipline that has helped her maintain a straight path in her career. Her father, a retired U. S. Marine Colonel, taught her to give 100% in everything.

About barriers to becoming the first female captain at the Pensacola Police Department and how that was received in a male-dominated profession, Kristin candidly stated "I've truly never had a problem." She said that she has always been treated fairly and with kindness. She added that, if anything, she has always felt the need to explain the rationale behind her decisions. "People always say that females make decisions from their hearts rather than from logic. Maybe it's me, but I have always felt the need to give a reason as to why I made a decision."

Captain Kristin Brown

In addition to ushering a new era of policing (female command staff) to the Pensacola Police Department, Kristin Brown has also brought a new level of professionalism. As an officer, sergeant, lieutenant, and captain, she has always performed professionally. It is often difficult for a police officer to keep his or her personal opinions and feelings from interfering with the decisions and actions he or she must take. However, Kristin does that. She conducts police business without her personal feelings getting in the way. She is a true professional.

END OF WATCH

Police officers are called daily to handle problems — which they do daily. So, nothing lets the wind out of the sails of a department like the death of one of its own. A whole department of officers cannot handle the problem. There is nothing to be done, except grieve. However, most departments can give a send-off second-to-none! Uniforms, formation, salutes, flags, rifles, bagpipes, bugles, and escorts — there is nothing like it. Seldom have I ever seen a dry eye when the last call is given. Here is how it works:

At the gravesite after the funeral, the words are spoken over the casket, the flag is folded and presented to the family, the rifle salute is conducted, bagpipes are played, and Taps are played by the bugler. Then, every officer who has their police radio on turns it up for all to hear. On the main radio channel where all officers are listening, the dispatcher calls the number of the officer, as if summoning him to respond to a call.

"Unit 45?" No answer.

A second call "Unit 45?" No answer.

A third call "Headquarters to Unit 45?" Still no answer.

"Unit 45 is 10-7 (finished for duty). May you rest in peace. We have the watch."

Something unforgettable to witness.

End of Watch: John William Robert Gordon: September 22, 1889

When a police officer dies, the whole community feels the effect. When an officer is killed in the line a duty, a strange phenomenon occurs. The citizens in the community feel a loss, and the department members feel like a member of their family has died. The members of the Pensacola Police Department had never experienced this feeling until September 23, 1889. It was the first time.

On February 14, 1885, the 16 police officers who were on the department's payroll at the time made history. They were officially listed as police officers when the state of Florida and the City of Pensacola reorganized. Officer Gordon earned $60 every month, or about $15 a week. Four years later, Gordon was still on the job, working his foot beat as normal. On September 22, 1889, Officer Gordon arrested David Sheehan. However, Sheehan resisted violently. Shortly after the arrest, Sheehan posted bond and was let out while awaiting his appearance in court.

The next day, Officer Gordon was working his usual foot beat at Palafox and Zarragossa Streets at 6:30 pm when he was approached by David Sheehan. Sheehan had been drinking at the bar called "Smarts" with his friend Tom Mullens most of the day. When they left the bar, Sheehan and Mullens walked up Palafox Street where they ran into Captain Jonathan Stokes and Captain Collins in front of Dannheisser's store, 410 South Palafox. Further up Palafox is where Sheehan came near Officer Gordon and accused Gordon of striking him unnecessarily. Officer Gordon explained that he was just doing his duty, then encouraged him to leave, but Sheehan refused and continued his accusations, becoming more agitated. Suddenly, Sheehan produced a firearm, causing Gordon to take cover and blow his whistle as a call for backup. He also drew his service weapon and fired. After at least five rounds were fired, Officer Gordon had been struck in the left side of the chest, the bullet passing through his heart, and exiting near his left arm pit. He staggered into nearby Sheppard's Drug Store, collapsed, and died 20 minutes later. Officers quickly arrived on the scene and Officer Hutchinson took Sheehan into custody. Officer Gordon, 35, was from Alabama and had two children, who received his pension. On December 20, 1889, David Sheehan was found not guilty of the murder of Officer Gordon. Following the coroner's inquest, Officer Gordon's body was shipped to Alabama for burial.

End of Watch: John G. Yelverton: June 1, 1899

As the town approached the 20th century, the growing pains for Pensacola had remained quiet. It had been 10 years since a police officer had been killed, and the mood was mostly festive. But then…law and order took a turn for the worse on June 1, 1899. Rueben Harris was wanted in Georgia for a shooting. After the shooting incident in Georgia, Harris fled to Pensacola on a train. Georgia Detective Thomas Watts and a deputy followed him and were present when Harris got off the train at Alcaniz and Wright. They watched him as he proceeded south on Tarragona Street from the train station. Following Harris, Detective Watts noticed Officer Yelverton, identified himself, and motioned for him to stop Harris.

Yelverton followed Harris to the corner of Tarragona and Chase Streets and approached him in front of the Stratton Ice Works. Harris pulled a revolver and fired three rounds into Officer Yelverton. One struck him in the head and another to his right side, mortally wounding him. As he fell, the wounded officer drew his revolver and shot at Harris, who had turned to run.

However, before Harris could flee, Detective Watts and the deputy arrived and each fired, striking Harris in the lungs. Harris ran behind the Stratton Ice Works building and hid. A few minutes later, Pensacola Police Chief Frank Wilde arrived and, together with the Georgia officers, began searching for Harris. Chief Wilde found him, armed with two pistols. Before Harris could shoot, Wilde subdued him and took him into custody.

Officer Yelverton was immediately taken to the Pensacola Infirmary where he underwent emergency surgery. Unfortunately, the surgery was unsuccessful. Officer Yelverton succumbed to his injuries on June 3, 1899. He left his wife, Ida, to mourn his death.

As to Harris, his condition — wounded in his lung — did not initially look good. However, he began to slowly improve. A few days later, he was moved to the jail infirmary. Citizens of Pensacola became enraged. Talk began about forming a lynching party. This threat became so real that Sheriff George Smith, who oversaw the jail, stationed specially armed deputies at the jail around the clock.

On December 5, 1899, Harris' murder trial took place. Harris' attorney argued that the shooting was an accident, but the jury returned with a guilty verdict. Harris was sentenced to hang, much to the approval of the community. However, On January 26, 1900, Governor William Bloxham allowed the State Board of Parole to commute Harris' sentence to life in prison.

End of Watch: William B. Burnham: March 17, 1908

On the evening of March 17, 1906, the weather was clear and mild — a typical March evening for Pensacola. W.S. Norman's Saloon was its usual busy, bustling self — typical for a Saturday. Most of the noises coming from the bar on the corner of Tarragona and Wright Streets were from laughing, happy, drinking men. This was a popular hangout for African American men who lived and worked in downtown Pensacola. They all knew each other, and most were friends, including one of the regulars, Jerry Lenox. On this night, however, a stranger came in. No one knew James Ardis, where he lived, or why he was in Pensacola. From the time he arrived at the saloon, he started to annoy people — seemingly on purpose. He started conversations which turned to arguments, as if he wanted to fight. He was looking for it. Then he confronted Jerry Lenox. Jerry had had enough of him and told him so. From there, Ardis and Jerry took it outside. Jerry grew tired of Ardis' mouth and decided that a fistfight might be the answer. However, he was not prepared for what happened next. Suddenly, Ardis pulled a handgun. This was no longer fisticuffs — this was serious.

Officer William Burnham was one of the best. Next to Charles Neel, he had made the most arrests of any of the officers at the police department last year — 338. That equates to almost one arrest every day. He knew his beat well. After all, this is where he spent most of his waking hours. He was hired almost three years prior when he was 28 years old and had proven himself since then. Last year, he caught the sailor who robbed the woman on Main Street. He and Captain Fondebilla raided a lucrative card game in the back room of the bar on Railroad Street. Also, it was he who arrested Leo Lee, the sailor from the USS Alabama who struck and killed Walter Mann last April on Zarragossa Street. He did his job well, and he loved it.

As Officer Burnham was walking his beat near the southeast corner of Wright and Tarragona close to the Union Depot, he saw what looked like an altercation in front of Norman's Saloon. As he got closer, he could see that a fight was breaking out between two men on the sidewalk. He started that way to break it up, but as he got closer, he noticed that one of the men had pulled a gun. The man shot twice at the other, but missed, as the targeted man ducked back into the bar. Burnham then called to the shooter and ordered him to put the gun down, informing him that he was under arrest. The man turned and fired at Officer Burnham, striking him in the chest.

With a bullet in his chest, Officer Burnham chased after the suspect, who fled east on Wright Street toward Hayne Street. Officer Burnham pursued him for less than a block before he stopped — he could go no further. He leaned against a telegraph pole for a few moments, then fell face forward. Several people ran to his assistance, including Sheriff Van Pelt, who had responded to the sound of gunshots. Officer Burnham tried to speak to the sheriff, but was unable, and died within a few minutes. The bullet had severed an artery in his chest.

After interviewing bar patrons and witnesses in the area, officers established the identity of the suspect as 25-year-old James Ardis of Pensacola. He had been in trouble before and had recently been released from prison after serving time for another shooting in the nearby Goulding community. Witnesses described him as being mean and dangerous, especially when drinking. He was known to always carry a .32 caliber revolver with him, which was consistent with the evidence. Officer determined that, on the night of the shooting, Ardis fled east on Wright Street, turned north, stopped at two businesses, and attempted to buy more ammunition. He was never seen again

Two days later, Officer Burnham's funeral was attended by hundreds. He was laid to rest in St. Michael's Cemetery. He was survived by his wife and two daughters. The Burnham family lived in the 500 block of West Government Street.

End of Watch: William Thomas Etheridge: December 26, 1908

William Thomas Etheridge was born on July 30, 1851 in Conecuh County, Alabama. On November 12, 1871, he married Nannie Bradley. They had three daughters: Clara, Ella, and Willie.

The first mention of him as a Pensacola police officer came on January 10, 1902, when he temporarily went undercover to catch burglars. On April 21, Officer Etheridge was attacked by a suspect armed with a knife. The suspect choked Etheridge and injured the officer's hand. On April 16, 1904, he was one of a few Pensacola police officers who were attacked by a large mob in retaliation for another officer making an arrest. In the aftermath of the hurricane of 1906, Etheridge broke his arm, but continued to work at his post until he could be relieved. Later that year, he was promoted to the rank of captain.

On Friday night, December 18, 1908, Captain Etheridge was patrolling on horseback when the horse stepped into a hole and fell, throwing the captain off. When the horse fell, it landed on Etheridge's arm, breaking it. After a few days, lockjaw (tetanus) set in. On the night of Saturday, December 26, Captain William T. Etheridge died from his injuries.

The funeral took place the next afternoon. It began at 3:00 at his home at 914 N. Palafox Street and continued to St. John's Cemetery where the interment took place. Rev. Charles Gavin of the First Methodist Church conducted the service. Pall Bearers were: Mayor C. C. Goodman, Alderman J. N. Andrews, Marshal F. D. Sanders, Chairman of the Board of Public Safety John Oliver, Dave Rutherford, and O. E. McReynolds.

End of Watch: J. H. Carter: April 4, 1909

Law and order. That's what it is called — for a reason. Historically, communities had often taken matters into their own hands when a horrendous crime took place. That sounds great, but not when emotions took priority over justice. For instance, if a person was accused of a terrible crime, a lynching might take place, often without the whole story being told. Occasionally, innocent people were wrongly killed. Such was the case in many towns, including Pensacola.

Officers who have worked the midnight shift will describe it as a different animal. Busy at times, slow at others, but always different. A city changes somewhat when most people are asleep. That's how it was at 1:00 am on April 4, 1909. 24-year-old mounted policeman Officer J. H. Carter was working in the Hawkshaw neighborhood on the east side of town — near 9th Avenue and Aragon Street. As a result of an unknown incident, Officer Carter took a man into custody. Officer Carter needed to have the man picked up by the wagon and taken to the jail. As they approached the patrol call box on the corner of Aragon and Luke's Alley, a fight ensued. The suspect stabbed Officer Carter multiple times, the fatal one in the chest, leaving a gaping hole. Before he collapsed, Officer Carter managed to fire two shots at the suspect. Carter died on the spot. Within a few minutes, Marshal Sanders, Captain George Hall, and Sheriff VanPelt arrived and began an unsuccessful search for the unknown suspect.

A few minutes later, a lady appeared at the desk sergeant's office at the police station inquiring about the bond amount for her husband, David Alexander, who had just been arrested by a mounted police officer (incidentally, another David Alexander was named chief of the Pensacola Police in 2015). Mrs. Alexander had been made aware that her husband had been taken into custody a few minutes before. Immediately, all officers were notified and sent to Mr. Alexander's home to contact him. When they first contacted him, Alexander's clothes were disheveled, and his clothing and countenance were consistent with being in a struggle. He was arrested and taken to the city jail.

Captain Hall testified later that Mr. Alexander had confessed to the killing of Officer Carter to him and Turnkey Charles Simpson. At the early stages, it looked as if Alexander was Officer Carter's killer, but the full story would never come out. Desk Sergeant Michael J. Murphy later testified that, at 4:00 am, 40–50 masked men stormed the city jail and accosted him and Turnkey Simpson, who were the only two men on duty at the station at that hour. They overpowered Sgt. Murphy, put him to the ground, and held him there. They then proceeded to Simpson and, holding a gun on him, made him open Alexander's cell door. They tied up Alexander and dragged him out of the jail and across the street into Ferdinand Plaza. They threw a rope over a pole, put the other end around Alexander's neck, and lynched him. Then, as he was hanging, they fired numerous bullets at him, fifteen striking him. The coroner later ruled the gunshots as the cause of death.

No matter how you view it, this incident was sad. One of Pensacola's finest had just been brutally murdered while doing his job, and his co-workers had worked swiftly and diligently to apprehend the man responsible. However, instead of the town mourning Officer Carter's death and proudly proclaiming the efficiency of the work of the department, a bunch of citizens allowed their emotions to get the best of them and put to death a man who had not been convicted of the crime.

Questions about the incident remain to this day. First, although Mr. Alexander's appearance looked like he had been involved in a struggle, there was no mention of blood on him. However, a large amount of blood was found on Officer Carter's clothing and at the scene. If Alexander had been involved in the killing, one would expect a lot of blood — or at least a little — to be on him. Apparently, there was no resistance on Alexander's part — not even an attempt to avoid being detected when officers came to his home. Also, no written statement of Alexander's confession existed; the only evidence was Captain Hall's testimony, which stated that he and Turnkey Simpson had heard Alexander confess to killing Officer Carter. In addition, Turnkey Simpson was also the one who was forced to unlock the cell when the mob came for Alexander. According to the testimony of at least one unconnected prisoner, none of the lynching party wore masks (as was stated in the official report) and when the cell door was opened, Simpson bade Alexander goodbye. Further, there was no mention of any other officers being summoned to assist when the two officers at the station were overrun. Even after the lynching took place and the gunshots were fired, no help was requested. According to individual accounts, instead of moving to stop the mob, other officers anticipated the arrival of the lynching party.

No one was surprised when Alexander was killed. An investigation into the lynching led to the arrest on April 17, 1909 of William "Russian Bill" Thompson at his home at Baylen and Cedar Streets. While awaiting trial, the jail personnel were increased for security purposes. On April 28, 1909, Thompson was found not guilty in a jury trial. As horrendous as this incident was, it is a credit to a town who cared as deeply for their officers as those of Pensacola did. However, vigilante justice is never the proper action. Did David Alexander kill Officer Carter? Maybe, but we will never know for sure.

End of Watch: C. Frank Bazzell: March 17, 1932

March 14, 1932: Finally! After four years as a firefighter, Frank was at last a motorcycle officer again. He had been a motorcycle officer in the town of Palm Beach, Florida, but since he had come to Pensacola, he was only now been able to secure the position with the Pensacola Police Department. On his first day, Frank Bazzell's assigned partner was Officer F. F. McDaniels, and they began their shift at 4 PM. It was a quiet evening, which gave Officer McDaniels an opportunity to show Frank around. Shortly after 10:00 PM, the officers received Frank's first call as a Pensacola Police officer. They were dispatched to a disturbance at the corner of 9th Avenue and Chase Street. As they were passing the intersection of Palafox and Garden Streets at 10:15 PM, Officer Bazzell's tire struck the curb, causing him to crash. Due to the urgency of the call, Officer McDaniels continued his response to the call. Upon his arrival, Officer McDaniels discovered that the call was a false one. Frank Bazzell lay in the street with a fractured skull and was transported to the Pensacola Hospital. He never regained consciousness. At 12:40 PM on March 16, 1932, Officer Frank Bazzell died from his injuries. The person who made the false disturbance call was never charged. Officer Bazzell was survived by his wife and 3-year-old son, Frank, Jr. The funeral took place on Thursday afternoon, March 17 at 4:15 PM at 1150 North 12th Avenue, the home of Mrs. C. C. Hartman. The burial took place at St. John's Cemetery. Pallbearers were members of the Pensacola Police Department and the Pensacola Fire Department.

The 324 most Heartbreaking Days in the History of the PPD

Family. Police officers are not simply considered co-workers to each other. Members are more like family, mostly because they must depend on each other in life-threatening situations. When two cops spend a lot of time together, they get to know each other well. They know about each other's childhood, parents, beliefs, spouses, children, plans. They also get to know what each other will do in a stressful situation. One cop might hang back and let the other do the talking. Another might be the one that jumps right in the middle of things. While one might run his mouth too much and end up starting trouble, another one might create a calming effect. Regardless, cops become close, because they spend a lot of time — a lot of dangerous time — together. The love and closeness cops have for each other extends beyond the cops themselves. What matters to one often becomes important to others. The children of one officer are often "taken under the wings" of the rest of the cops. If one officer finds the child of another doing something he shouldn't be doing, he most likely will intervene, or at least let the parent know.

The Pensacola Police Department circa 1945

When someone hurts an officer, or the family of an officer, personal feelings are felt against the 'outsider' who did the hurting. If someone injures or kills one of their own, the rest of the members of a police department take it to heart. That is why the days from February 26, 1938 to January 15, 1939 are the saddest days in the history of the Pensacola Police Department.

End of Watch: Clinton Augustus Green: February 26, 1938

He was born in Butler County, Alabama, near Greenville. When he was twenty years old, he decided that he wanted to get away, so he moved to Pensacola and became a deputy sheriff. After proving that he was a quality officer, he was hired as a Constable in District Two. Soon, he applied for the position of detective with the Louisville and Nashville Railroad. At age 34, he was hired as a Pensacola police officer. In 1937, he again proved himself and was promoted to motorcycle officer. He was known as a gentlemanly officer. In early February 1938, Officer Green heard about the young 6-year-old girl dying of leukemia in Pensacola Hospital He immediately donated blood.

On Saturday afternoon, February 26, 1938, Officer Green was working on his police motorcycle at his home when he received a call about a fire on Lee Street between 7th and 8th Avenues. Incidentally, the fire call was less than a block from his house at 1410 N. Eighth Avenue. He responded. After finishing with the call, he left, heading west on Blount Street. J. W. Alford, an employee with Southern Bell Telephone and Telegraph Company, lived at 1011 East Jackson Street. Mr. Alford was driving East on Blount Street when he turned left onto Hayne Street. However, he failed to see Officer Green heading West. His vehicle collided with Officer Green's motorcycle. Witnesses said that the policeman hit Alford's windshield and flew over the car. Besides a badly cut neck and internal injuries, he suffered from a fractured skull. He never regained consciousness. At 6:55 PM, Officer C. A. Green died from his injuries.

Officer Clinton Green

Officer Green left behind a wife, one son and four daughters. Funeral services were conducted Sunday afternoon, February 27 in his home. Reverend Chester S. Hunnicutt delivered the eulogy and brother officers served as pallbearers. The burial took place in Clopton Cemetery at Davis Highway and Selina Street.

A quickly assembled coroner's jury went to the scene of the accident and determined that Alford apparently swerved into Officer Green's path thereby causing his death. He was arrested on one count of manslaughter and turned over to county authorities where he was released on a $1,500 bond.

End of Watch: William Archie Bowman: August 19, 1938

Thirty-seven years. He had been in law enforcement in West Florida since 1901, serving first as a deputy, then nineteen years with the Pensacola Police Department as an officer and a special officer. William Archie Bowman was a veteran. If anyone knew police work, it was Archie. So, it was a real treat on Friday, August 19, 1938 for his nephew to go with him and watch him work.

During the shift, Officer Bowman responded to a call regarding articles taken from a vehicle at Tarragona and Wright Streets. His investigation led him to the residence at 1005 N. Davis Street. When he entered to house, he proceeded to the back room, but told his nephew, Henry Harvey, to stay in the front. Suddenly, Henry overheard angry voices. A man said something about being tired of the police always looking for liquor. Henry, who was thirteen years old, heard four shots, and a man with a pistol in his hand ran past him outside, got into a car, and sped away. A check on Officer Bowman found him lying face up in the back room with four bullet wounds in the chest, right arm, abdomen, and right arm.

Within a few minutes, police officers blanketed the area and Officer Bowman was rushed to the hospital by ambulance. He died on the way. Chief O'Connell ordered all officers to join in on a massive manhunt for the suspect, who had been identified as Ben Davis, 36.

The entire community was in shock, still mourning the loss of Officer Green, who had died six short months earlier. Flags were lowered to half-staff. All available officers — from all nearby agencies — began an intensive search for the suspect. Davis's vehicle was found in the Walnut Hill area in the far north end of the county. However, the suspect was not located.

Officer Bowman lived with his wife, Carrie, at 1816 West Government Street. He had one daughter, Mrs. J. B. Harris of Molino, Florida. Funeral services were held Sunday August 21 at 9 AM at the Bowman home. It was attended by one of the largest congregations in the city's history, according to the Pensacola News Journal report. After the service, the funeral procession, which stretched ½ mile, proceeded to Ray's Chapel Cemetery in McDavid, Florida where the burial took place. Pallbearers were officers of the Pensacola Police Department.

The search for the suspect widened, and descriptions were sent to all nearby cities in Florida and Alabama. Several unsuccessful leads were followed up before a call was made on August 25 to Chief O'Connell from the Uriah, Alabama officials. Davis had arrived at the home of a friend and hidden there. While there, he admitted that he had shot Officer Bowman. A private detective in Uriah overheard the admission and volunteered to transport Davis out of the area and the suspect agreed. Instead of taking him out of the area, he turned him in to the authorities. Davis was placed under arrest and transported to Pensacola for trial.

The prosecution had built a solid case against the suspect for murder, and it took only 15 minutes for a guilty verdict to be reached on January 18, 1939. Judge A. G. Campbell sentenced Davis to life in prison.

End of Watch: Herbert M. "Tommie" Hatcher: January 15, 1939

Officer Arthur T. Bobe, Jr. was a proud Pensacola police officer. In 1936, he was the first officer to be hired after the new civil service exams were set in place by the city. Officer Bobe and his family lived on the corner of Alcaniz and Chase Streets in downtown Pensacola.

Bobe's son, Arthur T. Bobe III, was called "Junior." He was 18 years old and a quiet boy. J. H. Workman was the principal at Pensacola High School where Junior attended. Workman described Junior as "an easy going fellow who never gave any trouble or caused any disciplinary action." As with any teenager, his mother and father loved him and tried to provide for him, including giving him with some spending money occasionally. Little did they know, however, that their son had a dark side. During the Christmas break, Junior talked of quitting school and joining the U. S. Navy. A few days later, he left home, but returned after the money ran out. These actions were strange for the quiet, unassuming young man. Officer and Mrs. Bobe never let on that they suspected any trouble. That is why they didn't suspect anything on the evening of January 14, 1939, when he told them that he was going to a dance.

Officer Tommie Hatcher

The Palafox Inn sat on the corner of Flomaton Highway (Palafox) and Scott Street. It is not known if Junior attended a dance that evening, but he did visit the Palafox Inn and caused a disturbance, which caused him to become angry. As he was leaving, he told clerk Glenn Wallace that he was going to get a gun and would be back to kill him. He left and went across the street to Gilmore's Service Station, where he confronted the attendant and asked if there was any money in the cash register. When the attendant said there was, Junior said that he would return.

Herbert M. Hatcher, known to everyone as Tommie, was born in Knoxville, Tennessee in 1904. When he was 17 years old, he left home and moved to Pensacola, Florida, where he worked at a bakery and with the Pensacola Fire Department. In 1932, he joined the Pensacola Police Department, eventually working his way up to motorcycle officer. He had been in more than one motorcycle accident, injuring his right ankle as a result. He still wore the brace.

Officer Hatcher was a likeable guy, popular with the other officers and with the citizens of his town. He also had a desire to help kids in Pensacola. According to the January 16, 1939 edition of the *Pensacola News Journal*, he became the director for the School Patrol, affecting the lives of hundreds of boys throughout the city. Many young men looked up to the amiable officer, obviously considering him a role model. Legend also had it that Officer Hatcher helped start the "Knothole" gang in Pensacola. The "Knothole" gang consisted of a group of underprivileged boys who, because they couldn't afford tickets to baseball games at Legion Field, had to watch through knotholes in the fence. The official club was formed so local businessmen could pay for the boys' admittance.

A few minutes after midnight on January 15, The Peoples Café, located at 223 East Wright Street, had about 15 customers in it when a young man, who was dressed shabbily, entered the restaurant. He aimed a revolver at the customers and workers and said, "It's a holdup, put up your hands." When the entire restaurant didn't come to a standstill, the young man fired two rounds into the floor and yelled, "Be still, damn you!" After taking about $15.00 from the cash box, he said "Someone put some money into the nickelodeon and start dancing." A passerby observed the incident from outside and flagged down Captain Riley Simmons and Officer Hatcher, who were patrolling nearby. Captain Simmons, who was driving, responded. As they arrived, Hatcher jumped from the patrol car and ran inside just as the suspect was coming out. They met just inside the door. As they faced each other, the young man shot Hatcher twice in the abdomen. He then bent down and took Hatcher's gun from his hand. Simmons approached and, seeing the event unfold, hastily fired one shot that missed the suspect, who opened fire with both guns on Captain Simmons. Simmons took aim through

Captain Riley Simmons

the front plate glass window and fired twice. One round struck the suspect in the head and the other in the chest. He was dead before he hit the floor. Simmons ran to Hatcher's side and checked on him, then summoned an ambulance.

As Captain Simmons turned his attention on the dead suspect, he took both revolvers. He immediately recognized one as belonging to Hatcher, but the other weapon — the one used by the suspect — also looked familiar. It looked like a police-issued handgun. Later, Chief O'Connell identified the gun. It belonged to Pensacola Police Officer Arthur T. Bobe. When detectives went to Bobe's home and woke him up in the night, they asked him to check if his duty weapon was there. He discovered it was gone. After the story was relayed to him, he accompanied officers to the mortuary and identified the body of his son. The sad situation of parents suddenly losing their son was enhanced by the knowledge of what their son had done. The Officer and Mrs. Bobe buried their son on Monday, January 15, in St. John's cemetery after a brief ceremony at their home.

Officer Hatcher was rushed to the hospital around 12:30 am. Emergency workers fought to save the brave officer but were not successful. Officer Tommie Hatcher died at 4:45 am.

Officer Hatcher was survived by his wife Eunice and their children — Herbert Jr., Tommie G., and Almedia Hatcher. The body was viewed on January 17th at Officer Hatcher's home, 926 E. Lloyd Street, then taken to Sacred Heart Church for the funeral service conducted by the Reverend Campodonica, pastor of Sacred Heart. The burial also took place at St. John's cemetery. Over 100 School Safety Patrol boys joined in the procession.

As uncomfortable as it was, many police department and city officials felt it necessary to attend both services — one for a slain police officer and the other for the slain son of a police officer. It was a terrible time for the Pensacola Police family.

End of Watch: Edward O'Brien Pursell: August 12, 1944

Edward Pursell never took music lessons. His family couldn't afford to pay for them. However, his talent helped him rise above his unfortunate circumstances and he taught himself to play the fiddle. After hours of practice and hard work, he became successful. Soon, he decided to enter competitions to match his talent with others…and he won! He went on to win several championships. Discussion soon followed about becoming a professional. Edward's answer was an emphatic "NO." His desire in life was to become a Pensacola police officer. That desire was fulfilled when he joined the force in 1943.

On August 9, 1944. Officers Purcell and H. P. (Buddy) Peake stopped Lt. A. D. Byers, U. S. N. on traffic charges. Byers immediately became abusive, cursing and using obscene language. After attempts to calm Byers, Officer Purcell placed him under arrest. During the arrest, the lieutenant violently resisted the officers, causing a physical fight. Suddenly, Officer Purcell grabbed his chest and collapsed from a heart attack. He was rushed to Pensacola Hospital and placed in an oxygen tent. After battling for his life for three days, Officer Purcell succumbed. To make matters worse, Lt. Byers filed a complaint on Officer Purcell for excessive use of force, denying the resistance or abusive language. Officer Purcell's funeral took place on Sunday, August 13 at 3:45 PM. The funeral began at his home on the corner of Garden and DeVilliers Streets and continued at 4:00 PM at the First Assembly of God Church, 1920 W. Garden Street. Officer Purcell had been a member of the Pensacola Police Department for almost a year. Interestingly, most officers and citizens of Pensacola were unaware of Edward Purcell's fiddle playing fame. He was buried at Union Hill cemetery in Myrtle Grove.

End of Watch: William "Bobo" Connors: September 16, 1944

Driving the patrol wagon was no easy task. It had a small wheelbase, it was top-heavy, and it was hard to maneuver. Choosing a driver was difficult, but it was a crucial part of the police process. When an officer made an arrest, he could call the patrol wagon to pick his arrestee up. This was done if the officer was on foot or on a motorcycle, in a detective car without a cage, or simply if the officer was busy and didn't have time to take the prisoner to the jail. The patrol wagon detail meant that the problem was left with the driver and his partner. Making prisoners comply, breaking up fights and getting them into the station were the jobs of the two officers assigned — usually veterans. The patrol wagon was also used to answer calls.

Pensacola Police Officers circa 1946

Such was the case on Saturday, September 16, 1944. Corporal William Henry Connors, 61 years old, had been a Pensacola police officer since 1921. William Connors was a favorite at the department. He was well liked, and always joking. But nobody knew him as William or Henry. He was "Bobo." Bobo Connors. Bobo was a second-generation Pensacola police officer. His father, William Connors, began his career with the department in the late 1800s.

On Saturday night, September 16, 1944, Bobo and Officer L.W. Taylor were partners driving the patrol wagon, working the 4 pm to midnight shift. Saturday night shifts were usually quite busy. At 7:45 pm, the desk sergeant's office received an emergency call from a West Government Street address. All patrol cars were busy, so the wagon was dispatched. Officers Connors and Taylor excitedly headed that way in a hurry — Connors was driving. As the big vehicle passed through the intersection of Baylen and Zarragossa Streets, Officer Connors suddenly slumped over the wheel, unresponsive. After attempts by Officer Taylor to revive Bobo were not successful, he immediately took the wheel and pulled the vehicle to the curb. He radioed that the patrol wagon could not respond to the call, and to send an ambulance to his location immediately. The ambulance that was owned by Waters and Hibberts Funeral Home arrived and loaded Officer Connors in it, then proceeded at breakneck speed to the Pensacola Hospital. Officer Connors died at 8 pm that night, presumably from heart failure.

Officer Connors left behind a wife, Daisy Walton Connors, two sons, William R., and George W. Connors, two daughters, Mrs. Frances Davis, and Miss Maxine Connors, two sisters and three grandchildren.

End of Watch: Louis Champa: May 26, 1951

Late Saturday night, May 26, 1951, motorcycle officers L. B. Morgan and Louis Champa were working around North Palafox Street, when a vehicle sped south past them. Champa and Morgan pursued. As soon as the vehicle passed the intersection of Palafox and Gonzalez Streets, another vehicle entered the intersection without halting at the stop sign. As soon as 31-year-old James Carl Davis realized his mistake, he slammed on the brakes. Unfortunately, he stopped directly in Champa's path — in the middle of the intersection. Champa tried to take evasive action, but the vehicle was too close and Champa's motorcycle struck the 1950 Buick solidly. Officer Champa was taken

Officer Louis J. Champa

by ambulance to Sacred Heart Hospital where he was pronounced dead. Davis was arrested for Manslaughter and held in jail. During the interview with Davis, he admitted to running the stop sign. He said that an occupant in his vehicle yelled to him to stop and he did, but directly in the path of Champa, leaving the officer no time to react.

Champa, a five-year veteran of the force, was born in Minnesota. He later moved to Cleveland and then to Pensacola in 1944. He and his wife, Vicki Louise Champa lived at 158 Aragon Court with their three daughters. Funeral services were held on Monday, May 28 at Fisher-Pou Funeral Home. Officer Champa was buried in full Pensacola Police Uniform with his fellow motorcycle officers serving as pall bearers.

End of Watch: James Jeffcoat: March 22, 1968

The front page of the June 10, 1951 edition of the *Pensacola News Journal* had a story entitled "Painter Kills His Baby Daughter in Family Fight." Richard Bonifay, a local painter, lived at 521 N. Spring Street. He was estranged from his wife, Jewell, and his 10-month old daughter, Linda Jean. On June 9, Bonifay came to the house of the Minton household, where Jewell and the baby had been staying. When Bonifay arrived, an argument ensued, and Bonifay became violent. The Mintons then heard a thumping noise repeatedly coming from the room the Bonifays were occupying. The Jewell Bonifay screamed "You have killed my baby!" As the Mintons rushed into the room, Bonifay said "I hope I did."

Bonifay was arrested and turned over to Detective James Jeffcoat. The veteran detective was smart, reserved and considered quiet and no-nonsense. However, he was not afraid or indecisive. He began a conversation with Bonifay and allowed him to speak what was on his mind, which he did, giving some vital testimony. At trial, Bonifay decided he had no option but to plead guilty. He was sentenced by Judge E. E. Mason to life in prison in Raiford, Florida.

James Jeffcoat was born in the small community of Caryville, Florida, but grew up in Pensacola. As a young man, he was a champion boxer in the Golden Gloves program. In 1941, he joined the U. S. Army and was sent overseas, serving during WWII. He spent 46 months in the European Theatre, including storming the beaches of Normandy on June 6, 1944. After the war, he immediately joined the Pensacola Police force in 1946. He served as a patrolman for five years, being promoted to sergeant in 1951. On April 25, 1961, he began his job as a detective after his promotion to the rank.

James Jeffcoat enjoyed raising pigeons in his spare time. His expertise came in handy one Saturday in 1957 when a pigeon flew into one of the windows of the police station. After the fowl waddled into Captain Raymond Harper's office, Sergeant Jeffcoat responded to a call from the good captain and correctly discovered that the bird was from New Orleans but could not fly home due to oil on its wings. The expert took the bird home, cleaned it up, and contacted the owner.

As a sergeant, Jeffcoat was known all over town, especially the west side of town, as the guy that oversaw all day-to-day police matters. He was instrumental in arrests, traffic crashes, and calls for help. He was everywhere! As a detective, he was involved in many cases, ranging from murders to burglaries.

On Friday morning, March 22, 1968, Detective Jeffcoat arrived at work as usual, and faced a busy workload at his office. Around 3 pm, he collapsed on the table in the detective's meeting room. His fellow officers immediately called for an ambulance and together, they carried him downstairs where they were met by emergency workers. Detective Jeffcoat was pronounced dead on his arrival at Sacred Heart Hospital.

Jeffcoat was survived by his wife and two daughters. They lived on Springhill Drive in Pensacola and attended First Methodist Church, where the funeral was held on March 24, 1968. He is buried in St. John's cemetery.

End of Watch: Curtis Neal Jones: June 27, 1980

It was early in the morning — the quiet time — of Friday, June 27, 1980. Officers Richard Powers and Curtis Jones were enjoying a cup of coffee together. At 5:30 AM, a call came over the radio calling for help from a deputy of the Escambia County Sheriff's Office at the scene of a burglary in progress at the Oar Lounge on Barrancas Avenue. Both officers immediately jumped into their vehicles and sped south on Palafox Street to respond. Jones was driving a two-month old 1980 Ford LTD. Recently the LTD models had been the subject of a national debate about the tires being substandard at high rates of speed. As both officers were headed down Palafox Street, Powers stopped at a red light, but Jones continued, driving 60–70 miles per hour. Rick Powers couldn't see down the hill on Palafox Street, but he could see the spectacular display of fire as Officer Jones' car cut the power pole in half. When Powers arrived at the scene, he could tell that Jones had been approaching Yonge Street when his cruiser veered off the road. The car snapped the power pole and bounced off the building at 2401 N. Palafox Street before crashing into the Palafox Lounge. Officer Jones never regained consciousness, and he died shortly thereafter. It appeared that Jones lost control after his vehicle struck a curb or the tires malfunctioned. The issue regarding the substandard tires was debated, but nothing was ever proven.

Officer Curtis Jones

Curtis was from Crestview, Florida, where he was survived by his parents, Mr. & Mrs. Valton Jones. Before joining the force three years earlier, he was an officer with the Crestview Police Department. Funeral services were held at 11 am on Monday, June 30 at the First Baptist Church of Crestview, where 150 officers attended. Members of the Pensacola Police Department served as the honor guard.

End of Watch: Amos Cross: September 12, 1980

Amos Cross, a native of Adel, GA, had spent 20 years in the U. S. Air Force as a police security supervisor for the Strategic Air Command. When he retired, he, his wife Margaret and three sons moved to 4216 Acacia Drive in Pensacola. In April 1979, he joined the Pensacola Police Department.

Many people described Amos Cross as a quiet, polite model of a man. He wanted to be a police officer to help others make their lives better. After enrolling in the police academy, he proved that he was also very intelligent and studious. Not only did he score exceedingly high on his grades, but he helped others in the class who struggled. When graduation time came, Amos graduated first in his class. Immediately after graduation, he was hired by the Pensacola Police Department. In less than a year on the force, he was put to the test on February 20, 1980, at a hotel room that had been purposely set on fire. Amos promptly extinguished the blaze in a matter of minutes. On May 29, 1980, Amos encountered a difficult decision. A man attacked another officer with a butcher knife. Amos could have legally shot the man but chose instead to talk him into a surrender. Amos became was a true hero, and he was popular on his beat. He was well-liked by the other officers as well as the citizens in the area his worked. They knew him to be a good, honest man.

Officer Amos Cross

Amos Cross knew Peter Todd well. He had been called to Peter's home when he and his father were arguing. He had spoken with him and calmed him down several times. He was like that. So, on Friday, September 12, he wasn't too worried when, at 7 PM, he was called to 610 N. "D" Street, the home of the Todd family. After all, he had been there several times in the past few weeks. In less than a minute, Officer Cross, 39, arrived at their home. The home was located between Jackson and Gadsden Streets, across from the Antioch Baptist church. On this evening, choir practice was in session at the church, and 50 children were in attendance.

Amos expected to calm the family down once again, as he had done in the past. Little did he know that Peter Todd was standing inside the front door with a loaded 12-gauge shotgun pointed at Amos. As the Officer approached the front door, Peter fired the shotgun, striking Amos in the face and killing him instantly. Todd then fled on foot, jumping the fence, and heading for the church, shotgun in hand. Officer Gary Cutler, who was a new rookie officer, arrived just as Amos was approaching the door. He witnessed the tragic event. As Todd fled, Cutler pursued, and caught up to him. The two exchanged gunfire. A bullet struck Todd in the head, causing him to drop the shotgun as he fell to the ground. Officer Cutler, who had also been shot and wounded, took Todd into custody. A search of the residence located Peter's father, B. J. Todd, whose lifeless body was lying in the back yard with a shotgun wound.

Funeral services for Officer Amos Cross were held on Tuesday, September 16, 1980, at the chapel on Corry Naval Air Station. The honor guard was provided by members of the Pensacola Police Department. For members of the police department, it had been 77 short days since the death of Curtis Jones, and the wounds were still fresh. The funeral procession to the burial site at Barrancas National Cemetery stretched for a mile, mostly due to police cars from numerous departments. They had come to show their respect for a true hero.

End of Watch: Stephen Taylor: October 19, 1982

Tuesday, October 19, 1982, was a beautiful autumn day in downtown Pensacola. The sunlight was bright, and the temperature was comfortable. Downtown Pensacola was its usual buzz of activity — shopping, doing business, driving, and walking. Suddenly, the silent bank alarm went off at the Freedom Savings and Loan Association at the corner of Palafox and Gregory Streets. Not that anyone thought the alarm was real, as most were accidental. The Pensacola police dispatcher assigned Officers Larry Bailly and Steve Taylor to the call. They arrived within seconds and covered the exits. A few seconds later, 18-year-old Cliff Jackson exited the building on Palafox Street with a bag full of money and a gun. He was immediately ordered to the ground to be taken into custody.

Unknown to the officers, Jackson's partner, Clarence Hill, 24, left the bank through the other exit and crept east toward Palafox Street. As Officer Taylor was bent over handcuffing Jackson, Hill walked up behind him and pulled the trigger, striking Taylor in the head and back. One bullet entered Taylor's body beneath his bullet proof vest and traveled upward, slashing through his internal organs. Officer Bailly, who was shot by Hill in the neck, pulled his revolver and shot all his rounds at Hill, striking him twice. Both offenders then fled the scene on foot. Jackson ran north to the corner of the bank, then west, away from shooting officers. Officer T.C. Miller arrived and ordered Jackson to stop. Jackson ignored the warning and continued, so Officer Miller shot him. He was caught and taken into custody a block away at a garage. Meanwhile, Clarence Hill ran across Palafox Street and behind the Dainty Del restaurant, where he was shot several times by Pensacola Police Sergeant Paul Muller. Both men were taken into custody and transported to the hospital. After being released from the hospital, they were kept at the Escambia County Jail until trial.

Officer Stephen Taylor

Cliff Jackson received a life sentence. Because Clarence Hill pulled the trigger of the gun that killed Officer Taylor, he received the death penalty. In January 2006, he was set to receive a lethal injection, but the U.S. Supreme Court gave him a stay of execution. The case was sent back to the Florida Supreme Court, which declined to hear the case. On September 20, 2006, Clarence Hill received a lethal injection and was pronounced dead at 6:12 pm. He had no last statements.

End of Watch: Glenn Rowe Austraw: February 26, 1997

Rowe Austraw was an intelligent, likeable young man. Everyone wanted to be around him. His confidence gave the impression he had more years than he did. He had wisdom beyond his years. Even though the class he was taking on February 26, 1997, was required, Rowe was anxious to learn more. He had quite a future ahead of him

George Stone Criminal Justice Training Center is located 9.4 miles from the Pensacola Police Department. It is the state of Florida's official training center for corrections and law enforcement for the state's Region One — the Pensacola area. A lot of the area's criminal justice training is held there. That is what Rowe Austraw was doing on Wednesday, February 26, 1997, driving to a class.

On February 26, 1997, Officer Austraw took his usual rout to class, Interstate 10 toward Pine Forest Road. Before he got to the exit, a tractor-trailer suddenly changed lanes in front of him, causing his truck to flip over several times in the median. The tractor-trailer fled the scene and was never apprehended. Rowe was pronounced dead at the scene.

Officer Austraw was survived by his expectant wife and his young son. His wife later gave birth to his daughter, born on his birthday.

THE PENSACOLA POLICE SHIELD

The author's badge – also worn by his father

The Pensacola Police Department has one of the most unique and attractive shields in existence. Officers, badge collectors and historians worldwide have attempted to purchase them. However, they are not for sale. The only way to possess one legally is to become a Pensacola Police officer. Here is a summary of the symbolism found in this great shield.

City Seal: The seal of the City of Pensacola is in the center of the shield. This is a unique but symbolic item. The first thing one notices is the round circle, the five different dates, the black hand and pen over the black shield, and the symbols inside the shield.

- The red color of the circle symbolizes military fortitude.
- The five dates represent the times that the city's charter was renewed.
- The hand stands for faith, sincerity, and justice.
- The pen symbolizes educated employment.
- The shield represents protection of citizens.
- The black color of the hand and shield stands for constancy.

The symbols inside the shield are a cross and crown. These symbols represent the mission that De Luna was on when he first settled in Pensacola to spread the Gospel of Jesus Christ and claim the area for the Spanish crown.

The "Pensacola" Banner: A banner with "Pensacola" is displayed across the middle of the shield. This banner symbolizes the city's reward for its long and rich valiant service. The blue color of the banner represents loyalty and truth.

The Five Flags: Pensacola is known as "The City of Five Flags" because during its history, the city came under the rule of five governments: Spain, France, Great Britain, the Confederacy, and the United States.

The Laurel Leaves: The laurel leaves on each side of the shield under the banner stand for the peace and triumph that Pensacola enjoys in its rich heritage.

The Eagle: The eagle at the top of the badge is a symbol of power and sovereignty.

For Pensacola police officers, this symbolizes the courage and freedom for which they fight. Each officer must earn the right to wear the shield, and each one wears it proudly.

CONCLUSION

The average Pensacola police officer encounters enough bizarre and life-threatening events to write a riveting action novel. The high-speed chases, burglaries, household disputes, death investigations — the police have seen it all. For many centuries, the little corner of the world, along the northern coast of the Gulf of Mexico has seen many inhabitants. As the population increased, crime escalated as well, creating the necessity for an effective law enforcement. The Pensacola Police Department has served its citizen through the city's rich history. Pensacola's finest carry on the tradition of excellence through protecting those around them, creating a legacy for others to follow.

As any officer who has five years' experience will tell you, they have enough unique experiences and have been through enough fires to write a book. The necessity of enforcing the rules and laws in any community has been around as long as communities have. For many centuries, the little corner of the world along the northern coast of the Gulf of Mexico has seen many inhabitants. And, whenever people live together, law and order become essential. As civilizations developed, the idea of appointing someone enforce the laws honestly and with equity became more common. That practice still exists today in the city of Pensacola through the officers and employees of the Pensacola Police Department. While the necessity of policing has caused the enforcers to "try and keep up," they have also managed to carry on a tradition of excellence — a legacy for others to follow.

REFERENCES

Pensacola, Spaniards to Space Age
Hagler Field, A History of Pensacola's Airport
Pensacola in Pictures and Prints
The Emergence of a City in the Modern South; Pensacola, 1900–1945
Minutes, Pensacola City Council
Minutes, Pensacola City Commission
Minutes, Pensacola Board of Public Safety meetings
Pensacola Police Department records
Pensacola Historical Society files
Pensacola City Hall records
Success Beyond Expectations; The Panton-Leslie Trading Company
John C. Pace Library files
West Florida Regional Library files
Andrew Jackson and Pensacola
Colonial Pensacola
Ante-bellum Pensacola and the Military Presence
Pensacola, the Deep Water City
Pensacola, the Old and the New
Letters from Pensacola, Descriptive and Historical
Pensacola: Florida's First Place City
Siege: The Battle of Pensacola
Pensacola News Journal
Newspapers.com
Pensacola Gazette

Interviews From:

Chief David Alexander
Chief John Mathis
Chief Norman Chapman
Chief Louis Goss
Chief James Davis
Chief D. P. Caldwell
Inspector Aldo Rasponi
Mrs. Clyde Touart
Detective Ted Chamberlain
Lt. Charlie DeCosta
Officer Jeri Schadee
Officer Randy Rickard
Sgt. Henry Cassady
Lt. Terry Ausborn
Elton Killam, Esquire

Lt. Dixie Chancellor
Sgt. Mike Wilkinson
Officer Mack Cramer
Sgt. Alfred "Skip" Bollens
Sgt. Jim Andrews
Officer Carlos Padilla
Lt. Greg Moody
Officer Scott Pelham
Sgt. Rick Steele
Officer Wes Cummings
Lt. Mike Maney
Officer Lamar Pate
Officer Bill Chavers
Officer Cliff Lyster

Footnotes:

1. *Pensacola Then & Now 1559-2016*
   http://www.pensacolathenandnow.com/1559-1821.html
2. *Florida Department of State, Division of Historical Resources*
   http://apps.flheritage.com/markers/markers.cfm?ID=escambia
3. *Lachlan McGillivray, Indian Trader* p. 425
4. Prevost to the secretary at war, September 7, 1763, *ibid.*, pp. 136-137
5. *British West Florida 1763–1783* pp. 27, 55, 69, 86-91, 162
6. *Pensacola: Spaniards to Space Age* p 51, 52
7. http://www.flheritage.com/facts/history/summary/
8. *National Park Service website:*
9. http://www.nps.gov/nr/travel/american_latino_heritage/Plaza_Ferdinand_VII.html
10. *The Supreme Court of Florida and its Predecessor Courts*, p33:
11. https://books.google.com/books?id=6DZsiFB1Oj8C&pg=PA30&lpg=PA30&dq
    =1821+judge+henry+brackenridge&source=bl&ots=AyOtpo3FUU&sig=-lupahs

K8PwM_ugDY3-vVWKJvJQ&hl=en&sa=X&ved=0ahUKEwjarabg-bbKAhVCgj4KHW5aADQQ6AEIJjAC#v=onepage&q=1821%20judge%20henry%20brackenridge&f=false

12. *Temporary Organization of Pensacola by Governor Jackson*, p. 16:

13. http://www.rootsweb.ancestry.com/~flwfgs/1999-20-Footprints.pdf

14. *The Papers of Andrew Jackson, 1821–1824*, p. 96

15. https://books.google.com/books?id=lBedSM3L4qIC&pg=PA96&lpg=PA96&dq=jackson+callava&source=bl&ots=3z-1kgrZuN&sig=kBwKw06l4G4DrEu9s-IiV5YkZAQ&hl=en&sa=X&ved=0ahUKEwjM9pzxgLfKAhVGcD4KHTcvAKMQ6AEILTAD#v=snippet&q=callava&f=false

16. http://dos.myflorida.com/florida-facts/florida-history/a-brief-history/civil-war-and-reconstruction/

17. The Evolution of Rural Justice in New Spain, culminating in the Acordata, and Attempts by the Spanish Crown to Institute the Tribunal in Peru by Barbara Gilbreath Montgomery, p 9.

18. https://ecommons.luc.edu/cgi/viewcontent.cgi?referer=https://www.google.com/&httpsredir=1&article=2408&context=luc_diss

19. https://fsu.digital.flvc.org/islandora/object/fsu:181720/datastream/PDF/view
p 51 & 52

Michael Simmons

ABOUT THE AUTHOR

The Pensacola police department has been a large part of my life. For many years, I have worn the badge with honor. A lot of other department members feel the same. I would like this honor to continue, which is the reason I wrote this book. I hope it has brought delightful reading to you!

www.ingramcontent.com/pod-product-compliance
Lightning Source LLC
LaVergne TN
LVHW051520070426
835507LV00023B/3220